GREEN INTERIOR DESIGN

LORI DENNIS

Allworth Press
New York

Published by Allworth Press, an imprint of Allworth Communications, Inc., 10 East 23rd Street, New York, NY 10010.

14 13 12 11 10   5 4 3 2 1

Cover design by Kristina Critchlow
Book design/typography by Mary Belibasakis
ISBN: 978-1-58115-745-1
Library of Congress Cataloging-in-Publication Data

Dennis, Lori.
  Green interior design / Lori Dennis.
      p. cm.
  Includes index.
  ISBN 978-1-58115-745-1 (pbk. : alk. paper)
  1. Interior decoration--Environmental aspects. I. Title.
  NK2113.D48 2010
  747--dc22
                                    2010022220

Printed in Thailand

CONTENTS

1 INTRODUCTION

I am an interior designer who began practicing green behavior as a child, long before I knew it was a movement. Being raised by a struggling, single mother and a grandmother who lived through the Great Depression, I was taught to conserve energy, never waste, and recycle. My mother honored the Cherokee part of our heritage, and respect for the planet was a core value I also learned at a young age.

The power of interior design captured my attention when I was four. We didn't have a lot of things or money. My sad, little bedroom consisted of a cot and a few secondhand toys. One day a package from my aunt arrived. It contained colorful Popeye sheets. I was thrilled and immediately ran to make the bed. Thirty-five years later I still remember the vivid transformation these bold, happy, comic strip sheets made in the dreary room. After that experience, the decoration and design of spaces captivated me. Everywhere I went I examined details of landscape, architecture, fabrics, and wall covers dreaming of the day I could be a part of these creations.

WHY DID I DECIDE TO WRITE THIS BOOK?

Years later, when I started my interior design firm it seemed logical to marry my agenda of green living with the concept of designing sustainably. I began searching for and specifying the limited amount of green products and concepts that were available ten years ago. Somehow I always seemed to gravitate to green people and became friendly with sustainable chef Jeffrey Mora, a big supporter of NRDC and Oceania. Some of his good friends include Jean-Michel Cousteau, Ed Begley Jr., Leslie Hoffman (executive director of Earth Pledge), and Ted Danson. He introduced me to these major leaguers of "green" and I knew I had finally found my niche in life.

Being a sustainable design firm means that we always include an aspect of green in every project we do. Our approach includes being mindful of how we use resources (materials and energy) while designing an aesthetically pleasing, highly functioning, and health-based environment. Because we are well known for our expertise in eco-friendly design, most of our clients request that we implement our green game plan into their interiors. The stage at which we enter a project and the budget usually determine how far we can go in a sustainable direction. As with traditional interior design, the sooner we are brought into a project, the more positive impact we can make. We make every argument for intelligent designs and well-planned spaces that efficiently use materials and do not waste square footage. We believe that good design is green design and things that last for many lifetimes are things worth buying. Our clients are encouraged to buy less, but buy the best they can afford. At our firm the concepts of luxury and green co-exist. Our definition of luxury, however, isn't having a lot of things—it is valuing quality over quantity. The quality we are talking about is organic, renewable, recyclable, healthy, and beautiful. We believe this is a timeless way to design.

As eco-friendly interior products and building materials continue to evolve daily, our goal is to learn all we can. This process includes trial and error; attending several lectures and open houses every week; reading Web sites, books, blogs, and magazines; exchanging information with sustainable players, vendors, and clients; and attending conferences and trade shows related to sustainable living. Over the past two years, I've seen more and more people—designers, architects, and builders—show up at these events because they are interested in a greener way of doing business. At a recent sustainable living lecture given by Mary Cordaro, one of my colleagues asked Mary how she could learn everything she needed to know to go green. She asked, "Isn't there a book?" Mary and I looked at each other, smiled and spontaneously thought, if only it was that easy. We both decided it was time for this book to be written.

WHY GREEN? ENVIRONMENT AND HEALTH ISSUES IN DESIGN PROJECTS

A few years ago Leonardo DiCaprio and Cameron Diaz started driving hybrids. Al Gore came out with a movie about global warming and every other product manufacturer started claiming that they were going green. The Green Movement had begun! Right? Wrong. The truth is that this movement began about thirty years ago and took awhile to get some mainstream steam. If you were a kid in the '70s, like I was, you might remember your neighbor putting up solar panels to heat their hot tubs. Songs by Woodsy Owl telling us to "give a hoot, don't pollute" were unavoidable if you went to public school (which most of us did back then). I also remember some pretty long lines at the gas station because of problems with something called OPEC and then everyone trading in their huge cars for sub compacts. People cared about energy, the planet, and each other. We all lived in smaller dwellings, had less stuff, and were cautious about turning off the lights when we left a room and not "hanging out in front of the open fridge." Most of what we ate was purchased from within 100 miles of where we lived and it wasn't pumped up with fillers, steroids, chemicals, preservatives, and who knows what else. You could hitch a ride across the country without fearing for your life because the United States, even in big cities, felt more like a bunch of neighborhoods. There was a sense of conservation and community that was everywhere. The movement wasn't called "green" yet but instead was simply a consciousness about being responsible to something bigger than yourself.

But then the '80s came along, we didn't feel so broke anymore, and everyone started consuming (food, products, resources, energy) without regard for how we were going to pay for it economically or environmentally. A few of those "conservationists" kept beating their Mother Earth drums, but most people forgot where they came from and failed to listen or worse told them to unbraid their leg hair and shave. Gordon Gecko from the movie *Wall Street* and Donald Trump spoke loudly about being greedy, much louder than the tree huggers, and people liked what they were selling a lot better. We lost touch of our sense of community when we no longer needed to go to public recreation rooms, parks, and pools. Our houses became so big that we had everything we needed all to ourselves. And of course, we felt the need to fill up these big houses and yards with lots of stuff, so we had to manufacture more and more for less and less. Everything became disposable and cheaper to buy new than to fix. Years ago I remember bringing a relatively expensive camera in for repair and they literally told me to throw it out and buy a new one, because it would cost less. I was shocked and a little disgusted. Even with all the means available to me at that point, I remembered what it felt like to have nothing and never wanting to waste what I considered to be valuable resources.

This consuming frenzy continued until the fall of 2008. Virgin resources were stripped from the earth, factories manufactured with little concern for the pollution they caused, cheap toxic products were shipped by the billions across the world, wrapped in excessive, fancy packages, with no regard for how they were to be handled after they were finished being used. This behavior has literally made our planet and us sick.

So now going green sounds pretty good. When you're sick and running out of resources, it makes sense to return to healthy approaches and conservation. Everyone has heard about being green and millions of people are trying it out to see if it works for them. While I welcome you to jump in with both feet, be careful not to overdose. My advice for getting started is don't try to learn everything on your first project. Many designers and builders have been doing things a certain way for so long, it seems almost impossible to begin making changes. The amount of information is overwhelming to digest all at once. Thinking you can completely change to a sustainable way of being overnight is like joining a gym and wanting to have a body builder physique the next day. Remember that no project (or any built structure) is 100 percent green, not even mine. Try implementing some of the things you learn as you design your next project and improve on each subsequent project. The most important thing to know is that training is critical. In addition to reading this book and the suggested additional reading, you must attend green building seminars, use experienced green contractors and trades, and train your team as you learn and practice. Feel confident that as you learn more about the subject, forming new eco-friendly behaviors is just a matter of repeating them over and over. After time, they will become second nature.

Manufacturers and vendors are making it easier for you to begin by offering thousands of green choices. Currently eco-friendly products are part of an industry with sales in the hundreds of billions, growing annually in double digits. And every time you buy something, you vote with your dollars. Vendors who don't offer green products are being forced to evaluate their product lines and marketing strategies so they won't miss out on a huge base of eco conscious customers. This has brought down the price for sustainable products considerably. I'd be lying if I told you all the products are as cheap as the mass produced goods that usually come from China (with little or no regard to what effect the materials and manufacturing have on our planet and health). As the demand for green products grows, however, the prices will continue to drop. So if you have to buy, buy green. I like to think of a time in the near future when we don't need to specify "green" anymore. Things will just be made with consideration for the environment and our health as common practice.

WHAT IS "GREEN"?

Green is a term used to describe products or practices that have little or no harmful effects to the environment or human health. Most people have heard about recycling by this point, but don't realize that the products they use have an effect on the environment from the point of extraction to manufacturing, shipping, packaging, use, and finally disposal. Green companies seek to find products that are derived from renewable sources with minimal impact on the location of extraction. Care is taken in the manufacturing of the product not to add toxic ingredients that are harmful to human health or the environment in production, i.e. chemical additives that will be dumped into a nearby waterway or landfill. Consideration is given to using recycled materials in the product composition. The distance and method of shipping should be as benign as possible. When packaging a product, they choose environmentally friendly materials and as use as little as possible to protect the product from the point of shipping to the consumer. Green products can also be made with regard to the end of their useful life and companies may give instructions how, why and where to recycle or dispose of them properly. Another aspect of a green company is what they do with their success. How are the employees treated? How are profits divided? How does the community at large or the consumer who supports them benefit?

A traditional product or company focuses on providing a product that performs safely with the goal of making a profit. Green companies and products have the same agenda but also take into account how they are impacting the earth and human health and well-being. The goals of a green product or manufacturer are to preserve and protect air, water, soil, wildlife, waterways, and food supplies by being conservative with natural resources and producing less toxins and waste. They also strive to improve human conditions by giving back part of the profits they generate to communities and people in need.

INTERNAL CHECKLIST

The biggest sustainability challenge facing designers today is understanding how the products they select truly impact energy use, the environment, and health. Understandably one of the first things people do when determining what to purchase is look at what products are made of and how easy they are to recycle. But rarely does one stop to think about the manufacturing process, transportation, or the installation of products. For example, a few years ago I attended a lecture put on by Donghia for Pollack fabric. During the presentation, they introduced a few green fabrics that were new to their line. The representative from Pollack discussed the recycled materials that went into the product and the fact that the factory was environmentally responsible, but didn't seem to think it was a problem that the fabric needed to be shipped from Switzerland. When I brought up this point, his answer was, "Well, we need to start somewhere."

I agree with him. But where do we start? And how do we measure how green something is or isn't? It's already complicated enough to select beautiful, appropriate, and green items. To add another layer to the selection process—is it green enough?—makes the design process even more difficult. Fortunately, as the green movement becomes more mainstream and more industries join the movement, it is getting easier. We are now seeing eco labels and ratings on products and projects. These labels help us to determine characteristics of products: whether they contain recycled materials, whether the manufacturer uses resources and energy efficiently, how much pollution a product generates in its lifespan, any health concerns, water conservation, whether it can contribute to LEED points and many more green qualifiers. You may have seen the Energy Star Rated symbol on appliances you've specified lately or the Water Sense label on plumbing fixtures. LEED rated buildings are also popping up all over the place—I'm sure you've heard about or seen them. I've included a glossary at the end of this chapter to help you decipher what these labels and rating systems mean to you and your projects.

At my firm, we have two internal checklists we use when we begin a new project: the client/property checklist and the product checklist. As any good designer should, we thoroughly interview our clients about the obvious (what does the client want and need) and then go into the not-so-obvious areas of their personal health and green aspects of their project. Remodeling or new construction can be driven by many factors. The client may need more useable space. The space the client is in may contain outdated or worn furnishings and materials. Health concerns like allergies or asthma might play a role in the decision to make changes.

The following client/property checklist of questions helps us to determine how best to design in an environmentally friendly, health based way that addresses the client's needs and allows them to live well in their new space.

INTERNAL CLIENT CHECKLIST

Client Health

- Is the client experiencing coughing, sneezing, chronic fatigue, asthma, frequent headaches, dizziness, or any other unexplained symptoms?

- Are these symptoms exacerbated by prolonged periods indoors?

- Do these symptoms disappear when they leave for extended periods and return when they come home?

- Are they aware of any mold? Humidity? Musty odors or mildew? Do houseplants have mold?

Reasons
- Why has the client decided to begin this project?
- Why have they selected a green interior design firm? For environment or health reasons?
- How long do they plan to live in the newly designed space?

Size
- How much space does the client need? Is it really necessary?
- What is occurring in these spaces?
- Does the space plan take advantage of all useable space?

Building Design
- How can we take advantage of natural light and airflow in most, if not all, of the entire residence?

Building Materials
- What are the client's aesthetic preferences?
- Does the client have health/chemical sensitivities to certain materials?
- Is there an opportunity to use salvaged materials?
- Does the owner have materials or furnishings that they wish to reuse?
- What are the owner's attitudes about cleaning and maintaining the property?

Insulation
- How can we seal the walls, ceilings, doors, and windows to prevent unwanted heat/cooling loss and gain?
- Is noise pollution a factor?

Energy Usage
- Are the home's systems efficient? This includes lighting, appliances, water heater, heating/cooling.
- Are current energy bills unusually high?

Renewable Energy
- Is there an option to install renewable energy systems? On what scale?

Water Conservation
- How can we minimize indoor water use and waste?
- Are there options for installing grey water systems?
- Are there options for rainwater collection?

Landscape
- What types of plantings are indigenous to the region?
- How can we minimize or eliminate non-porous hardscape?
- Is there an option for a green roof? Can it be used?
- How does the client feel about an edible or cutting garden?
- Can landscaping provide shade to south and west sides of the home?
- What are the opportunities for outdoor living spaces?

Once we have established a good understanding of the issues driving the project and we are ready to begin purchasing, we refer to our product checklist. The product checklist helps us to make the most sustainable choices by measuring eco products against conventional products and against other eco products as well.

PRODUCT CHECKLIST

- Is it locally produced?
- Is it grown organically?
- Does it come from renewable sources?
- Are there extraction methods with little or no impact on the environment or wildlife?
- Is it made of recycled or reclaimed materials?
- Has it been produced without toxic chemicals or ingredients so it doesn't offgas or release toxins into the environment?
- During manufacturing were recycling methods used to eliminate waste?
- Does the manufacturing plant utilize energy saving systems?
- Is it packaged minimally?
- Is it good quality design that will last for a lifetime?
- Is it the most energy efficient type of product of its kind?
- Is it adaptable and can its life be extended to meet changing needs and tastes through upgrading or refurbishing?
- Can it be recycled at the end of its life?
- Does the manufacturer accept responsibility for taking back the product for refurbishing or recycling at the end of its useful life?
- Does it have a third party green label?

Very few, if any, products will have a favorable answer to each of these questions. But the more yes answers you have on your list, the more confident you will be that you are selecting truly green products.

CERTIFICATION

You may want to go the extra step and certify your project. In addition to the environmental and health benefits, certification may make your property more desirable and valuable to others. There may also be local, state, and federal financial incentives to certifying a project. The following is a list of North American green building certification programs and resources to help you achieve certification.

- **BuildingGreen** (*www.buildinggreen.com*) is an independent company committed to providing accurate, unbiased, and timely information designed to help building industry professionals.

- **Build It Green** (*www.builditgreen.org*) is a nonprofit membership organization with the mission of promoting healthy, energy- and resource-efficient building practices in California.

- **Built Green Canada** (*www.builtgreencanada.ca*) is an industry-driven voluntary program that promotes green building practices to reduce the impact building has on the environment.

- **Built Green Colorado** (*www.builtgreen.org*) encourages homebuilders, suppliers, and manufacturers to use technologies, products, and practices to build green homes that are better for the environment. Colorado has the nation's most successful building program with over 30,000 homes registered by 2005.

- **Built Green Washington** (*www.builtgreenwashington.org*) is a cooperative of Washington's regional green home building programs.

- **Chicago Green Home Program** (*www.ci.chi.il.us*) is a rating system in Chicago that is designed to encourage developers, builders, and homeowners to build and remodel green.

- **Earthcraft House** (*www.earthcrafthouse.com*) is a green building program that serves as a blueprint for healthy, comfortable homes that reduce utility bills and protect the environment.

- **Energy Star Qualified** (*www.energystar.gov/index.cfm?c=new_homes.hm_index*) in order to qualify a home must meet guidelines for energy efficiency set by the U.S. Environmental Protection Agency.

These homes are at least 15 percent more energy efficient than homes built to the 2004 International Residential Code and include additional energy-saving features that make them typically 20 to 30 percent more efficient than standard homes. Homes must include: effective insulation, high performance windows, tight construction and ducts, efficient heating and cooling equipment, efficient products, and third party verification. Any home three stories or less can earn the Energy Star label.

- **Florida Green Building Coalition, Inc.** (*www.floridagreenbuilding.org*) is a nonprofit corporation dedicated to improving the built environment.

- **LEED for Homes** (*www.greenhomeguide.org/green_home_programs/LEED_for_homes.html*) is the USGBC's rating system that promotes the design and construction of high-performance green homes. A green home uses less energy, water, and natural resources, creates less waste, and is healthier and more comfortable for occupants.

- **National Association of Home Builders** (*www.nahbgreen.org*) has voluntary Model Green Home Building Guidelines that are designed to move environmentally friendly home building concepts further into the mainstream marketplace.

- **The NC (North Carolina) Healthy Built Homes Program** (*www.healthybuilthomes.org*) provides a certificate for homes meeting "green home guidelines" built by residential builders who practice sustainable, high-performance building strategies making the home a comfortable, healthy, and affordable place that reduces energy and water usage, promotes renewable energy use, and helps protect the land where the home is built. In a HealthyBuilt Home, building materials and processes are selected to reduce pollution and the waste of natural resources during the manufacturing and construction phases and throughout the life of the home. The builder is encouraged to provide homeowner education about the high performance features of the home and provide local resources for "green" living.

- **REGREEN ASID** (*www.regreenprogram.org*) is the partnership of The American Society of Interior Designers Foundation and the U.S. Green Building Council for the development of the best practice guidelines for sustainable residential improvement projects. This program will increase understanding of sustainable renovation project practices and benefits among homeowners, residents, design professionals, product suppliers, and service providers to build both demand and industry capacity.

- **Santa Monica Green Building Program** (*www.buildinggreen.com*) is committed to protecting the environment, improving quality of life and promoting sustainability.

GLOSSARY

The glossary below will help equip you with a green vocabulary to begin enjoying the information in this book. Congratulations on your decision to make a positive change for our industry, the earth, and each other.

alternative energy energy derived from natural sources that can be renewed at the same rate it is used. Some examples include: sunlight, rain, tides, and geothermal heat.

American Society of Heating, Refrigeration, and Air-Conditioning Engineers (ASHRAE) advances technology to serve humanity and promote a sustainable world.

bau-biologie the study of how buildings affect human health. This knowledge is applied in green new construction, renovations, and remediation (fixing sick buildings).

biodegradable the ability of soluble chemicals to break down into nontoxic ingredients that can go back into the earth or water systems.

carbon neutral achieving net zero carbon emissions by balancing a measured amount of carbon release with an equivalent amount of offset.

carcinogen any substance or radiation that is an agent directly involved in the promotion of cancer.

carbon footprint the total set of greenhouse gas emissions caused directly and indirectly by an individual, organization, event, or product.

certified organic how the USDA defines organic production as a system that integrates cultural, biological, and mechanical practices that foster cycling of resources, promote ecological balance, and conserve biodiversity.

chlorofluorocarbon (CFC) widely used in aerosols, propellants, and refrigerants. They are believed to cause depletion of the ozone layer.

chlorine a poisonous toxin that takes many years to evaporate while in the earth or water.

clean energy a renewable energy source that does not pollute (wind, solar, geothermal, and hydrogen).

compost the decayed remains of organic matter that has rotted into a natural fertilizer.

composite boards are bonded waste wood from industrial processes or post-consumer recycled material that preferably contain no toxic materials.

Cradle to Cradle a rating system developed by William McDonough and Dr. Michael Braungart that assesses products on a number of criteria, such as the use of safe and healthy materials, design for material reuse and recycling, efficient use of energy and water throughout production, and instituting strategies for social responsibility.

DEA free does not contain DEA (diethanolamine), a substance linked to cancer.

dioxins a highly carcinogenic chemical by-product formed during manufacturing and incineration of other chemicals which bioaccumulate in humans and animals due to their fat solubility.

ecolabel a third party certification that attests the characteristic of a product and its low impact on the environment.

EcoLogo a third party certification of environmentally preferable products that was established in 1988.

emissions cap a limit placed on companies regarding the amount of greenhouse gases they can emit.

energy efficient a product that uses less energy than the same conventional product.

Energy Star an EPA rating system for products which use energy. Energy Star rated appliances meet the EPA's minimum energy efficient standards.

Environmental Protection Agency (EPA) an independent federal agency that was established to coordinate programs aimed at reducing pollution and protecting the environment.

fair trade an organized social movement that helps producers in developing countries promote sustainability. Living wages, environmental and social standards, and a move toward economic independence and stability are the movement's main goals.

formaldehyde a chemical carcinogen, known as a throat irritant and headache inducer.

Forest Stewardship Council (FSC) a nonprofit organization that sets certain high standards to ensure that forestry is practiced in an environmentally responsible and socially beneficial manner.

FSC certified a product label that means the wood used in the piece and the manufacturer that made it met the requirements of the FSC.

fuel cell a technology that uses an electrochemical process to convert energy into electrical power.

global warming an increase in the earth's atmospheric and oceanic temperatures widely predicted to occur due to an increase in the greenhouse effect resulting especially from pollution.

Global Organic Textile Standard (GOTS) aims to define requirements to ensure organic status of textiles, from harvesting of the raw materials to environmentally and socially responsible manufacturing to labelling in order to provide a credible assurance to the end consumer.

green philosophy supporting social, economic, and environmental sustainability.

green design a philosophy of designing the built environment with the principles of economic, social, and environmental sustainability.

green energy see clean energy

Green-e Power an independent, renewable energy certification and verification program allowing consumers to quickly identify environmentally superior energy options.

Greenguard a certification program run by the Greenguard Environmental Institute (GEI) which establishes acceptable indoor air quality standard for products.

greenwashing a superficial nod to the environment that marketers and businesses that historically were not interested in sustainable concerns are doing in order to improve their public relation standings with the consumer or public.

Green Seal is an independent and non-profit organization that evaluates and recommends products based on criteria that emphasize pollution prevention and environmentally responsible life cycle management. Eligible products are awarded the Green Seal.

grey water systems systems that treat household washwater (all waste water except toilet and garbage disposal) and reuse the water to irrigate landscaping and flush toilets.

heat island effect when heat islands form as vegetation is replaced by asphalt and concrete for roads, buildings, and other structures necessary to accommodate growing populations. These surfaces absorb rather than reflect the sun's heat, causing surface temperatures and overall ambient temperatures to rise.

Home Energy Rating System (HERS) a system that involves an analysis of a home's construction plans and onsite inspections. This analysis yields a projected, pre-construction HERS Index. This index is subject to inspections of actual conditions once the project is completed.

Intergovernmental Panel on Climate Changes (IPCC) the leading body for the assessment of climate change, established by the United Nations.

International Organization for Standardization (ISO) a third party agency that specifies requirements for environmental management systems and social responsibility pertaining to fabric manufacturing.

landfill an area designated to receive solid wastes, construction debris, household trash, and sludge from sewage treatment. A layer of soil is spread over the fill each day to reduce smell and health hazards. Well-run landfills are lined with plastic or clay to prevent toxins from entering the groundwater. Environmentalists dislike landfills because of their potential to pollute and the permanent removal of valuable raw materials.

Leadership in Energy and Environmental Design (LEED) a green building rating system with an independent certification program that provides voluntary guidelines for developing high performance, sustainable buildings. Created by the U.S. Green Building Council (USGBC), the program awards different levels of certification to buildings that meet LEED rating standards in five major catagories: sustainable development, water savings, energy efficiency, material selections, and indoor environmental quality.

light emitting diodes (LED lights) emit visible light when electricity is applied, much like a light bulb. LED lights use a fraction of the energy that fluorescent bulbs use to illuminate a space and they can last for decades without replacements.

life cycle the total impact of a system, function, product, or service from the extraction of raw materials through the end of its useful life.

living wage a term used to describe the minimum hourly wage necessary for a person to achieve a specific standard of living. This term generally means that a person who works a forty hour week, with no additional income, should be able to afford food, housing, utilities, healthcare, transport, and recreation. This term does not mean minimum wage, which is a number set by law that may fail to meet the requirements of a living wage.

low-e windows made of high performance glass designed to reduce glare and heat gain for energy efficient windows that offer clear views and energy savings.

No or low VOCs (volatile organic compounds) VOCs are found in paints, sealers, painting strippers, and other solvents including household cleaners. VOCs contribute to ground level ozone and smog. Products that are below legal limits for their product class are called low VOCs and products that test negative are called no VOCs.

non-renewable resources natural resources, like gas, coal, and oil, that once consumed cannot be replaced.

nontoxic ingredients which pose no health risk.

Oeko-Tex Standard 100 introduced to the textile industry in Europe, this third party agency specifies allowable levels in fabrics of potentially harmful substances that threaten human health.

offgas the term for the release of toxic gases from man-made materials.

organic a term meaning no synthetic or chemical pesticides were used in growing a crop.

Global Organic Textile Standards (GOTS) a requirement that is used to ensure the organic status of textiles, from the harvesting of raw materials through environmentally and socially responsible manufacturing, packaging, labeling, exploration, and distribution in order to provide a credible assurance to the end consumer.

ozone layer a naturally occurring, atmospheric layer, fifteen miles above the ocean, that forms a protective layer shielding the Earth from excess ultraviolet rays.

pesticides chemicals used to kill insects and microorganisms.

petrochemical a product made from petroleum.

phosphates chemicals found in dishwashing and laundry detergent. When they are released into the waterways via storm drains they can produce excess growth that depletes oxygen levels and harms or kills aquatic life.

photovoltaic panels solar panels that convert sunlight into electricity.

phthalates industrial chemicals (plasticizers) which are frequently added to products to make plastic more flexible. They are suspected to be carcinogenic and hormone disruptors.

post-consumer waste material that has been discarded after someone uses it.

pre-consumer waste material that has been discarded before it was ready for consumer use.

polyvinyl chloride (PVC) the third most widely used thermoplastic polymer. Plasticizers that must be added to make PVC flexible have been of particular concern because some of these chemicals leach out of the vinyl products and are extremely toxic. DEHP is one of the most common toxic phthalate additives as it is a suspected carcinogen and reproductive toxicant.

radiant heating a system that supplies heat directly to the floor. The system relies on heat transfer, the delivery of heat from the hot surface to the people or animals in the room.

reclaimed materials anything that was built and then reused for a new purpose.

recyclable a term to describe a product that after its intended use can be remade or manufactured into another useful material or product.

recycling the act of processing used materials into new raw materials.

refurbished the cleaning and reconditioning of useable parts.

renewable energy see clean energy

Restriction of Hazardous Substances (RoHS) the directive on the restriction of the use of certain hazardous substances in electrical and electronic equipment. This directive restricts the use of six hazardous materials in the manufacture of various types of electronic and electrical equipment. It is closely linked with the waste electrical and electronic equipment directive which sets collection, recycling, and recovery targets for electrical goods and is part of a legislative initiative to solve the problem of huge amounts of toxic e-waste.

Scientific Certification Systems (SCS) a leading third-party provider of certification, auditing, and testing services and standards, founded in 1984.

sick building syndrome a combination of ailments caused by exposure to toxins in a residence usually resulting from poor indoor air quality.

SKAL a well-respected Dutch nonprofit that certifies worldwide organic agriculture and production.

structured insulated panels (SIPS) a composite material consisting of two layers of structural board with insulation in between which share the same properties as an I-beam.

sustainable a term which means using a resource so it is not depleted or permanently damaged.

Sustainable Furniture Council a nonprofit organization of suppliers, manufactures, retailers, and designers formed to promote sustainable practices in the furniture industry.

triple bottom line sustainable business practice that involves the pursuit of three goals: economic profit, ecological integrity, and social equity instead of a single, financial bottom line.

Water Sense a partnership sponsored by the U.S. Environmental Protection Agency that makes it easy for

Americans to save water and protect the environment by labeling these products with a Water Sense logo.

United States Green Building Council (USGBC) a nonprofit community of leaders working to make green buildings available to everyone. Council members work together to develop industry standards, design, and construction practices as well as guidelines, operating practices, policy positions, and educational tools that support the adoption of sustainable design and building practices. Members also forge strategic alliances with industry and research organizations, federal government agencies, and state and local governments to transform the built environment. As the leading organization that represents the entire building industry on environmental building matters, USGBC's unique perspective and collective power enable members to effect change in the way buildings are designed, built, operated, and maintained. The USGBC's greatest strength is the diversity of its membership. USGBC is a balanced, consensus nonprofit organization representing the entire building industry, comprising more than 12,000 companies and organizations. Since its inception in 1993, USGBC has played a vital role in providing a leadership forum and a unique, integrating force for the building industry.

volatile organic compounds (VOCs) found in paints, sealers, paint strippers, and other solvents, including household cleaners, these VOCs contribute to ground level ozone and smog. Products that are below legal limits for their product class are called low VOCs and products which test negative are called no VOCs.

After you have put what you learn into practice and have designed an eco-friendly interior you will also have the responsibility of encouraging your clients to change their behaviors in ways that will reduce energy and create healthier homes. Teaching them practices like water conservation, using ceiling fans in conjunction with steady airflow instead of turning on the air conditioning, turning down the thermostat in the winter because you've ensured that the building has been properly insulated and windows and doors are sealed for efficiency, turning off lights when leaving a room or using natural light instead of artificial during the daytime, wiping feet off on a mat or simply removing shoes, and cleaning with environmentally friendly products will enable them to participate in an energy efficient and healthy lifestyle while enjoying the environment you have helped to create.

Remember, this information is probably new to them as well and while you may be well meaning, be careful not to be overbearing. Explain the benefits with a smile and perhaps even provide a written manual with specifics about their home. You can lead a horse to water and hopefully it will be thirsty enough to drink.

2 FURNITURE AND ACCESSORIES

Most conventional furniture and accessories on the market today are made overseas with little regard for the raw materials that are wastefully excavated, the pollution that is created during manufacturing, packaging and transport, or the unfair wages and working conditions many factory employees endure. A home is thought to be a haven, but if it is flooded with toxic materials, it's not exactly the idyllic retreat we imagine. Typically the wood, plastic, and fabric in most furniture is made or finished with toxic materials, so the furnishings selected to make a space livable actually create indoor air pollution that is harmful to human life.

Toxic chemicals and organic pollutants used in paints, paint strippers, and wood preservatives routinely applied to household furnishings are suspected to cause cancer in humans and animals. Formaldehyde, a known indoor pollutant, is used as an adhesive in most residential wood furniture. Polyurethane, a toxin known to cause cancer in humans, is used as a sealant in most residential wood furniture. Brominated flame retardants (PBDEs), linked to brain disorders and birth defects, are used extensively in household furniture, even though they have been banned throughout Europe. All of these factors contribute to Sick Building Syndrome, which can cause dry or burning sensations in the eyes, nose, and throat, headaches, dizziness, fatigue, nausea, and memory loss. By selecting furniture and accessories from companies that use renewable or sustainably grown, nontoxic materials, environmentally friendly manufacturing processes, and engage in fair trade practices you help to diminish environmental and health hazards, and you continue to make green products more available and affordable.

Bedroom by Lori Dennis, photo by Ken Hayden

When you have a stunning, sustainable piece that will last for many generations, you don't need to buy a new one. This Hollywood Hills bedroom is understated and grand all at once. Reclaimed railway ties add a lot of character to the bed.

significantly different interior style. By making alterations to her existing pieces she was able to reuse 95 percent of her furniture. The other 5 percent was sold at a yard sale and on Craigslist, and donated to a women's shelter. My client paid about one tenth of what she would have to buy new things and her house looks incredible. She was happy, I was happy, the planet was happy.

REUSE WHAT YOU HAVE

Before you run out and buy anything new, consider using what you already have. Look closely at what can be cleaned, refinished, painted, repurposed, or reupholstered. A client of mine recently moved into a new home with a

The chandelier in this entry hall had been in the client's mother's dining room for decades. After she downsized to a smaller living space, my client inherited it and designed the entry hall scale to accommodate the stunning fixture. Buying the same type of chandelier new would have cost a small fortune. He was delighted to reuse a piece that had been in his life for so many years.

BUY THE BEST

If you are going to select new pieces, make sure to buy the best, most durable furniture you can given your budget. When it comes to furnishing a home, buying things that are made to last, things that don't have to be replaced, is one of the greenest game plans you can have. When a piece of furniture can be passed down through generations it prevents the need for raw materials to take its place, as well as manufacturing and disposal. The advertising team at Sutherland Furniture says it best: "We hold the philosophy that the only thing better than recycling is to make something that never needs to be recycled." Today's purchases should be tomorrow's antiques.

Entry by Lori Dennis, photo by Ken Hayden

Cliff Spencer is a master craftsman who lives and breathes green. The husband and wife team gracefully sculpt future heirlooms from recycled materials (like this wine oak coffee table) and FSC or reclaimed woods as shown in the dresser featured on page 18.

SELECT GREEN MATERIALS

Choose furniture that is made with sustainable materials and little or no toxic finishes. There are many components to consider when making green choices for upholstered pieces, from the wood frames, glues, webbing, springs, foams, and cushions to the fabrics, each piece needs to be examined for sustainability and potential health hazards. Any wood element should be FSC certified from well-managed forests and fabrics should be sourced from eco-friendly products. Read labels before you purchase and ask a lot of questions. Ask questions to the point of being annoying. Some vendors think they are making a green piece of furniture when in reality 85 percent of the piece could be toxic and imported from a place where their workers are subjected to questionable labor environments.

When my daughter was born, I purchased a new sofa from a vendor I work with in Los Angeles. Since I knew I would be sitting on the sofa breastfeeding a newborn for a good portion of each day, it was crucial that this piece have few, if any toxins. Times being tough in the beginning of 2009 for the interiors business, I wanted to give the business to a friend of mine who manufactures upholstered goods. Prior to this purchase we had many conversations about him going green in his factory. I was excited for him to do this for many reasons, one being that I could specify his products.

My new sofa came home looking amazing, covered in the gorgeous organic cotton fabric I selected. But when I looked at the cushion content tag, I was so disappointed to see that the cushions were made of polyurethane—not exactly green. I realized that this was my fault. I had taken for granted that a furniture manufacturer who sincerely wanted to go green would understand all the components a locally made sofa needed to be green, including the way he manufactured, disposed of waste, and delivered. In order to get my good friend up to speed on the green future, I would have to painstakingly go through each process questioning what he was and wasn't capable and prepared to do. Learn from my mistake—ask about everything so there are no surprises.

NONTOXIC INGREDIENTS

A healthy living space is one that contains furnishings with nontoxic finishes. Instead of solvent based finishes, which offgas for years, choose water-based, no-VOC finishes. Foams are typically made with petroleum-based products which have been linked to hormone disruption. This is frightening when you think of all the time you spend with your skin touching and absorbing these materials. The glues and frames of upholstered pieces often contain noxious chemicals including formaldehyde. Lee Industries is a well-respected company that manufactures luxurious upholstered goods. For years they have run an ad campaign promoting their product as green. Specifically they state that their fabrics, foams and adhesives are nontoxic and their wood is FSC certified. However, I recently learned they only use approximately 13 percent sustainable products in their foam. So you see, it's really up to you to grill the manufacturer to be certain the cushions are made from non-petroleum based materials, the glues, adhesives, and finishes are free of PBDEs and formaldehydes, the fabrics are organic, durable, and easy to clean, and the wood is reclaimed or FSC certified.

FAIR TRADE

Unless we are buying from a local manufacturer, we don't usually think about the people who make our furniture. Many times these people are subjected to unhealthy work environments and risk their lives for a few dollars each day. It is imperative to buy from companies that practice fair and safe manufacturing processes. Because so many, unfortunately, do not, green companies will make it clear when they are practicing eco-friendly economic and social behavior—just read their environmental statements. Often you will be able to identify "the good guys" with a fair trade label. As an added bonus, companies that support local artisans and indigenous peoples tend to have unique furniture and accessories which greatly enhance room interiors.

Jane Grey of Stray Dog Lamps is a hero to the less fortunate. Instead of pumping out mass-produced items with no soul, she employs artisans in third world countries. Her company allows them to empower their communities by creating art and using techniques that have been passed down through generations. The result is accessory pieces that resonate with life, as each piece is hand made by someone who cherishes the experience. The Haitian artisans are especially grateful for the opportunity to prosper after repeated earthquakes almost devoured their land. As you can see from these photos, her products create whimsical, happy spaces that also enhance the lives of the occupants who enjoy them.

EASY TO CLEAN

Select furniture that is easy to keep clean. Well-maintained items will last longer and reduce the need for replacement. Dirt and dust free environments are also better for indoor air quality. Smooth, hard surfaces will be easier to clean than heavily detailed pieces. If you are in a humid climate, avoid furniture that will absorb moisture. Slipcovers and fabric window treatments should be made of washable fabric or materials. Buy furniture and accessories that do not require routine application of toxic products.

ERGONOMICALLY CORRECT

No matter how perfect it looks, resist the urge to purchase furniture that is not comfortable or ergonomically correct. I made this mistake in my home office. I went for the sexy looking chair and regretted it every time I had to sit in it. I sold it on Craigslist for a huge loss; at least the new owner loved it. Sitting and sleeping pieces need to look good and provide excellent support.

RECYCLE

I have never completed a project without searching at least one of the following: Craigslist, thrift shops, garage sales, consignment shops, antique stores, or eBay. Selecting salvaged, used, vintage, or antique pieces adds a charming quality to any interior. Depending on your budget, buying a used piece can be the most affordable or expensive purchase of your project. Either way, it will be the greenest. Make this a habit on every project. Collectively we will eliminate millions of pounds of furnishings from entering the waste stream. On the flip side, donate unwanted furnishings or give them away. Never throw them away.

Jane Grey living room

My client fell in love with these vintage, abalone inlaid, R.J. Gibbings dining table and chairs. He wasn't, however, in love with the $17,000 price tag. When we discussed the amount of joyful dining that could occur at the table over decades, however, the expense seemed more reasonable. After all, tables of this quality, in this condition, made by Mid-Century masters don't come along every day. Well kept, this table can become an investment that will likely appreciate in value.

Cliff Spencer dresser

ANTIQUE, VINTAGE, AND USED SOURCES

1stdibs *(www.1stdibs.com)* is an online marketplace where users can search and bid on the world's greatest decorative arts. What I love about this site is that even if you don't buy anything, you can search the site free of charge. The experience is like taking a semester course on the finest dealers of antiques, mid century, modern, vintage furniture, and lighting. The list of vendors represents the best from around the globe.

Former Furniture *(www.formerfurniture.com)* is an online consignment featuring Hollywood's A-list furniture. With styles ranging from contemporary to vintage to traditional, you are sure to find a gently used piece you love. You can shop or sell on the site.

Twenty Gauge *(www.twentygauge.com)* is located online and at the world famous H.D. Buttercup manutailer. Twenty Gauge offers refurbished metal furniture and accessories. Each piece is powder coated, a method that enables a piece to last for decades in any climate, without rusting. The powder coating releases a negligible amount

Of course not everyone can afford a $17,000 dining table. These vintage, rosewood table and chairs were purchased on eBay for about $1,500. It's just perfect for the client and can grow with his family, as it has a leaf and a total of six chairs.

Incorporating antiques into any interior adds an immediate feeling of history, especially in a newly built space. M.S. Rau has some of the most beautiful pieces I've ever seen, rivaling any European shop. If you ever get to New Orleans, make sure to visit them, as the smell and touch of these fine works of art are something that is impossible to capture in a catalog or website.

of VOCs and provides a finish coat that is resistant to chipping, scratching, and fading.

Twentieth *(www.twentieth.net)* is a 10,000 square foot showroom and exhibition space featuring contemporary and vintage design. Well-known international designers, in-house designs, as well as emerging talent are showcased in what has been called the most impressive collection of contemporary furniture outside of the Metropolitan Museum of Art.

Simply Mod *(www.simplymod.com)* sells affordable vintage finds.

Sotheby's *(www.sothebys.com)* features some of the world's most distinguished decorative arts. If you have the budget, I highly recommend attending a preview and auction for at least one piece in your career.

M.S. Rau Antiques *(www.rauantiques.com)* has been a French Quarter landmark for almost 100 years and has a remarkable collection of 30,000 square feet of fine art and 18th and 19th century decorative arts. They are so certain of their quality that every single antique they sell can be returned for the purchase price, plus a 5 percent appreciation for five years. And I thought Nordstrom had a good return policy.

eBay *(www.Ebay.com)* is an online auction site which contains everything you can imagine. Don't forget to use them as a resource for your furniture and accessory searches and as a place to sell items that don't make the final cut.

Craigslist *(www.craigslist.com)* is a Web site that allows consumers to post and review items for free. Individuals contact each other directly for transactions. Cities and countries from all over the world are represented.

Goodwill *(www.goodwill.org)* is the world's largest nonprofit provider of job training and employment services for disabled people. Many times Goodwill will pick up your donated items. Their auction site *www.shopgoodwill.com* offers over 11,000 bargains every day. Need to fill a library? This is a great resource.

Women's Shelters *(www.womenshelters.org)* features a comprehensive list of women's shelters throughout the United States. Find a shelter in your area and contact them for a list of what they need. Imagine how great it will feel to help a struggling family get their life back on track and clean out your clutter at the same time.

New life was sprayed onto this '40s vintage desk. The powder coat orange paint is virtually indestructible and brightens the day of anyone who sees it.

UPHOLSTERED PIECES

ABC Home (*www.abchome.com*) has focused on selling eco-friendly furnishings at a reasonable price for the last decade. Many of the items are made from recycled materials and sustainable or organic fabrics with respect for fair trade practices. The styles range from ultra modern to traditional and contain many unique artisan pieces.

Crate and Barrel's affordable younger sibling (*www.cb2.com*) sells a smaller-scale, urban upholstery line with eco-friendly construction and materials. Some features include: certified sustainable hardwood frames, soy based cushions, removable seat covers for cleaning, and organic fabrics. Their products are made in the United States.

Crate and Barrel (*www.crateandbarrel.com*) believes the best place to conserve and protect our natural resources is at home. Their American-made lines feature sustainable woods and renewable materials. They offer full-scale and smaller, apartment-sized furniture. The company is currently working on more eco-friendly initiatives in their product lines.

Cisco Brothers (*www.ciscobrothers.com*) is an American manufacturer that has practiced social responsibility since the early 1990s by renovating abandoned warehouses and providing apprentice/employment programs in inner cities. Their handmade furniture ranges in style from contemporary to traditional and every piece is built to last. They use responsibly grown wood frames, reclaimed wood legs, non toxic fasteners and finishes, petroleum-free latex cushions, and use organic or renewable fabrics colored with vegetable-based, low-impact dyes and laundered in chemical-free, vegetable-based detergents. The furniture is comfortable, attractive, and can be made custom.

Edward Ferrell + Lewis Mittman's Pure Collection (*www.ef-lm.com*) contains some of the most luxurious, well-made, transitional-style furniture available today. The company's long term sustainable initiatives include manufacturing goods in North Carolina, employing an American workforce, and eliminating millions of tons of greenhouse gases required for overseas transport. In their factory they have instituted a recycling and reuse program for excess materials and a water recycling system. The following sustainable materials are used in manufacturing: organic fabrics, soy-based cushions, low VOC paints, adhesives, and finishes, FSC woods and veneers, renewable fibers like jute twine, and recycled content nail heads.

Simply divine, stylish, well-made and affordably priced Mitchell Gold (*www.mitchellgold.com*) is a vendor with a green heart. They support a long list of charities. Most importantly they developed and run a day care model for American workers that rivals any European facility. The education-based center is a model for all American businesses with its superior equipment, learning, and nutrition plans. The company has been making eco-friendly furniture way before it was in vogue. Furniture is made from recycled content and nontoxic materials, including recycled and recyclable packaging.

Hudson Furniture (*www.hudsonfurnitureinc.com*) creates works of art from salvaged or storm damaged trees. The line offers beds, tables, case goods, upholstery, and sculptures finished with hand-rubbed oil. They are New York's only repository for petrified wood with legal authority from embassies and consulates where the wood was taken.

Furnature (*www.furnature.com*) has been making organic furniture since the early '90s. Their pieces are free of toxins, healthful for humans, and easy on the environment. Making affordable furniture that will last for many generations is one of their solutions to stop the poisoning of the Earth. They understand that environmental consciousness is no longer a choice but a necessity if we expect health and prosperity for future generations. This is also one of the few green manufacturers that offer traditional styles of upholstered pieces.

With showrooms all over the country and one in Dublin, Ireland, Environment (*www.environmentfurniture.com*) has some of the sexiest eco-chic furniture I've seen. Reclaimed woods, oil drums turned sculptures, and dining room tables made of old Brazilian phone poles make up some of the collection. Environment gives back to humanity by selling Haitian artwork that supports Brandaid, a cause to help artisan microenterprises.

The primary goal of Q Collection (*www.qcollection.com*) is the elimination of toxic chemicals, carcinogens, and all chemicals that add to indoor air pollution. They use only natural, non-toxic and biodegradable materials in their transitional, upholstered furniture. All of their hardwood has been certified by the FSC. All of their textiles are printed with low impact, heavy metal free dyes and their leather uses only vegetable dyes in the tanning process.

Ligne Roset (*www.ligne-roset-usa.com*) is a French modern upholstery company that has been practicing sustainability since the '70s. They begin with a clean, low-toxicity manufacturing environment and produce products that don't create pollution in the consumers' homes. The furniture contains no harmful solvents in finishings, no fungicides or biocides, no heavy metals, no formaldehyde, and no PBDEs or PBBs. Every piece is designed with thought given to how it can be recycled at the end of its life. The employees are French, so you can imagine how good they have it: cost-free at work nurseries, ergonomic workstations, machines which eliminate noise pollution, and a lot of paid vacation days!

Arktura *(www.arktura.com)* sells funky, futuristic furniture, housewares, and architectural products and is committed to the sustainable future of our environment by making products that last for lifetimes. The majority of their products are made using durable materials with high recycled content and are fully recyclable at the end of their lifetime. High quality, zero VOC products are used for finishing. The company practices sustainability in its solar and wind powered warehouses.

Lori Dennis *(www.loridennis.com)* is a retailer/design firm that allows anyone to "get the look" without the

Cisco brothers has been "doing sustainable" for well over a decade. They manufacture in refurbished warehouses, injecting desperately needed employment opportunities into depressed communities. When you look at the superior style of their transitional designs, you can't help but want a piece in your own home. They feel as good as they look and they last and last.

This sofa was headed for the trash because the client didn't like the color. It was worn and he wanted a more modern style. By simply recovering the worn, dated throw pillows and seat cushion with brightly colored, organic fabric, the client was thrilled and the sofa was saved from a landfill.

This sleek, modern sectional, containing organic materials including soy foam, allows you to enjoy a healthy lounging experience. Knowing it's made in the good old USA is an added bonus.

designer price tag or fees. Eco-friendly pieces range in style from modern to transitional. The founder literally wrote the book on green design and is forever researching the most sustainable sources and practices. The company donates generously to many charitable organizations including Smile Train, Children's Cancer, Doctor's Without Borders, Surf Rider Foundation, programs to feed, clothe, and shelter the needy, and just about anyone else who asks.

One of my favorite retailers, Ikea (www.ikea.com), has a never-ending list of socially and environmentally responsible acts. From recycling centers in stores, to non-toxic products, to flat pack shipping (which saves millions of tons of transportation-related greenhouse gases), to use of sustainable, recyclable, and renewable sources, to recycling food waste from its restaurants into energy sources, to powering plants with renewable energy sources, to donating products and money to charities throughout the world, to employing local artisans, to encouraging consumer conservation by not providing free plastic bags—

seriously, I could go on and on. They have excellent style and value for exceptional prices. And I'll let you in on a little secret: I use some Ikea products in every project I design, even in my most recent $14,000,000 residence.

In addition to a variety of environmentally sensitive upholstered pieces, Pottery Barn (*www.potterybarn.com*) offers a lightweight desk chair made of 100 percent recycled aluminum. It's rather attractive.

CASE GOODS AND TABLES

Eric Slayton (*www.ericslayton.com*) sells artistic pieces individually signed and made of recycled steel and reclaimed wood.

Boom (*www.boomusa.com*) believes that you should have nothing in your home that isn't functional and beautiful. Their products are developed from trees of sustainable forests and lacquers are all water based. The aluminum they use is 100 percent recycled and recyclable. Equally important is their respect for social well being; they do not associate with manufacturers that use child labor, they enforce American labor laws in all of their operations, and they pay their Thailand staff above national rates.

Samuel Moyer Furniture (*www.samuelmoyerfurniture.com*) is a small cohesive band of artists and artisans who are committed to making one of a kind furniture by hand from sustainable materials. They believe in creating furniture that links generations, reducing waste and consumption.

Cliff Spencer (*www.cliffspencer.net*) makes furniture and cabinets using old-world craftsmanship with the finest joinery, built to last for generations. This knowledgeable firm coaches their clients in making eco-friendly choices to support the future of our global environment. This Greenopia distinguished business works with walnut, cherry, maple, mesquite, elm, pacific coast maple, eucalyptus, and sycamore. They specify reclaimed lumber, backyard trees, and sustainable materials. Stains and finishes are water-based and low VOC.

At Sidecar Furniture (*www.sidecarfurniture.com*), David Johnson, a master craftsman, uses traditional woodworking techniques to create environmentally friendly pieces. He only uses sustainably harvested and reclaimed woods finished with natural and petrochemical-free products and nontoxic glue.

Thos. Moser (*thosmoser.com*) sells handmade, Craftsman style furniture made from sustainably harvested American Black Cherry trees in Pennsylvania. The furniture is joined with centuries old techniques which ensures it will last for generations. They offer a lifetime guarantee for the original owner.

Whit McLeod (*whitmcleod.com*) sells Arts and Crafts

furniture made from reclaimed and salvaged materials.

Using FSC wood is a good compromise, but consider alternatives like engineered and strand woven board. Kirei (*www.kireiusa.com*) uses strong, lightweight, durable, and environmentally friendly substitutes for furniture and cabinetry. Both their Kirei Board and Kirei Bamboo are recycled, come from renewable sources, and contain no formaldehyde in their adhesives. Using Kirei will also help you qualify for LEED points in your project.

OUTDOOR FURNITURE

In addition to all of the health and environmental concerns related to any piece of furniture, outdoor pieces present their own unique challenges because of the weather they are exposed to on a daily basis. It is important to select pieces that are extremely durable and able to last through multiple generations. The majority of outdoor furniture is made of virgin plastic material. Although it is water resistant, plastic has a tendency to break down in sunlight. Obviously this isn't a good choice for multigenerational items. Instead choose materials that will hold up to the elements. Teak and bamboo have natural water resistant properties and can withstand UV rays which makes them perfect candidates for any high moisture area like poolside, bathroom, cabanas, and home spas. Composite materials made from wood and recycled high-density polyethylene are also good choices for long-lasting exterior furniture. When outdoor furniture is not in use, it is important to cover it or move it indoors.

Henry Hall Designs (*www.henryhalldesigns.com*) keeps environmental impact low during production and uses recycled resins and sustainable woods. The highest quality materials and techniques are used resulting in long lasting products. In every factory, American or European, working conditions providing fair wages and safe conditions are standard.

Loll Designs (*www.lolldesigns.com*) sells a variety of hip outdoor styles from Adirondack to vintage to modern. They also have a scaled down line for children. A 1% for the Planet member, they practice sustainability in their manufacturing, including reclaimed waste water, wind power, recycling, and recycled content materials for products and packaging. The furniture is made in the U.S. and they plant a tree for each order they receive.

Poly-Wood, Inc. (*www.polywoodtrade.com*) specializes in high performance lumber substitutes made of high-density recycled plastics (HDPEs). This extremely durable furniture resembles natural wood but doesn't require the same painting, staining, or sealing maintenance of real wood.

Neoteric Home (*www.neoterichome.com*) has some of the most interesting and rarely seen designs in outdoor furnishings. These high-quality, high-density, polyethylene-based fibers (Viro and Rehau Raucord) are free of the toxic residues associated with most plastics yet look completely like natural fibers. The furniture is resistant to UV rays and moisture and has antimicrobial properties to resist mold and fungus.

Spruce *(www.sprucenola.com)* sells super stylish outdoor furniture with a sense of humor. When locating retail and design space, the best friend team renovated an old warehouse in New Orleans in an effort to bring much needed economic development to our beloved Big Easy.

ACCESSORIES AND HOUSEWARES

Buy fewer accessories. We Americans have a bad habit of buying too many things we really don't need to fill up houses that are too big. This has resulted in a huge debt problem and a vicious routine of carelessly consuming precious raw materials, polluting during production, packaging, and transportation, and incomprehensibly wasting valuable materials by adding these used up products to the waste stream. Not to mention, most accessories are made in countries where there is little or no regulation or regard for the health of workers, the consumer or the environment. Granted, accessories can be useful and lovely additions to any interior, so choose them carefully. Pay attention to what they are made of, how they are made, packaged, shipped and how they can be recycled or last for many lifetimes.

I have mixed feelings about the following sites. Yes, they have fabulous accessories but so many of these items are just plain unnecessary. Although green accessories are better than their mainstream competitors, it's still not good to buy a bunch of knick knacks and toys that won't be used after the novelty is gone. Be selective when considering any accessory. Unless it truly serves a purpose, is a vision of inspiration, or will last a lifetime, don't buy it, even if it is green.

Magazine editor Zem Joaquin *(www.ecofabulous.com)* shares information about every green product that hits the market. Written in blog form it is really a great big advertisement for all things eco. It's a very informative and fun site to visit.

Branch *(www.branchhome.com)* features furniture, bedding, lighting, home décor, and cute kids and pets stuff, all innovative, all green.

Spruce Eco Studio *(www.sprucenola.com)* has a site with a good number of products I regularly specify, like Eco Smart Fireplaces, fabrics, wall covers, linens, and

You never need to feel guilty buying used books to position as accessories. They cost next to nothing, look amazing, and give you something to do to pass the time. Casually drop them on any surface to gain a relaxing but intelligent looking interior.

other accessories. The site has a real funky look and the products don't disappoint.

Touch *(www.do-not-touch.com)* is a 1% for the Planet member and a collaboration of emerging designers who create handmade, environmentally friendly products.

Vepca *(www.vepca.com)* sells antique European posters.

Living Green *(www.livinggreen.com)* is run by Ellen Strickland, a pioneer in the green building industry. Their mission for the past 20 years has been to offer clients healthy and sustainable choices in building materials, finishes, and home furnishings.

VivaTerra *(www.vivaterra.com)* specializes in home and garden products handcrafted from organic and sustainable sources and designed well with respect for the planet.

Econscious Market *(www.econsciousmarket.com)* is a unique site that gives to charity every time you make a purchase and allows you to decide which one from a very, very long list. They offer furniture (for babies and kids too), accessories, lighting, clothing, housewares, sportswear, and body products. Additionally the site provides a blog type section with a plethora of green info. And of course, they are a 1% for the Planet member.

Crate and Barrel *(www.crateandbarrel.com)* offers a sea of intelligent and affordable designs to brighten any interior. A personal favorite is the Calypso Collection: glasses, pitchers, and bowls made of 100 percent recycled glass.

The Container Store *(www.containerstore.com)* has a

Media room by Lori Dennis, photo by Ken Hayden

The austere stone floor called out for something soft and sustainable to warm it up. Wool rugs, like the one seen in this photo, are naturally fire resistant and hold up to the toughest Super Bowl crowds. The sofa is made of Sensuede fabric which is made from recycled materials and spot cleans with a quick scrub of mild dish soap and water. Instead of turning up the heat, make throws accessible for a more cozy movie time.

line of Eco Gen bath accessories made from a polymer called PHBC that can decompose in less than a year.

RUGS

Area rugs are a more eco-friendly choice than wall-to-wall carpeting. When purchasing, select rugs that are made in environmentally and socially responsible ways, are created from renewable materials, or are antiques.

The Natural Carpet Company *(www.naturalcarpet-company.com)* is a manufacturer, importer, and exporter of unique natural fiber carpets including abaca, raffia, wool, silk, buri, hemp, bamboo, seagrass, cotton, and rattan.

Pure *(www.purerugs.com)* features a sophisticated collection of cowhide rugs. All hides are from cows in the food industry. Their tanneries are certified as being low impact for the environment and all rugs are biodegradable.

GoodWeave *(www.rugmark.org)* is an international foundation devoted to ending child labor by building schools and programs and creating opportunities for the nearly 300,000 children who are exploited in the rug industry. When you buy a rug from a *RugMark.org* vendor, you can be certain that no illegal child labor was used to produce it. The vendors supporting the foundation are some of the most well-known retailers in the world and the styles range from modern to traditional.

Helios Carpets *(www.helioscarpet.com)* offers beautiful wool carpets with recycled and recyclable plastic cores. The company practices eco-friendly efforts in their plants including grey waste water, low mercury light bulbs, green solvents for washing, and recycling yarn waste into a composite that is used for automobile mats. Excess wool is recycled into bionutrients for soil and all natural carpet pads.

ACCESSORY LIGHTING

The importance of artificial lighting design is often overlooked in residential interiors. In a green home, the lighting plan is critical because of the amount of energy it can potentially waste. When an interior has been well designed, natural light should flood the space during the day. With an abundance of natural light, you can space plan to take advantage of natural light so that artificial light only needs to be used at night. For example, place a desk or chair next to a window with lots of natural light. This will result in energy savings and a more pleasant daylight source.

For a successful lighting plan, there needs to be a good balance of ambient and task lighting. Indirect fluorescent lighting is a great eco-friendly, ambient source. Task lighting requires the lighting source to be directed precisely where it is needed. Frequently recessed or under counter lighting are used as task lighting sources. With innovations in lighting these sources can now be fluorescent or LED instead of incandescent.

Most lamps that historically used incandescent bulbs can be replaced with compact fluorescent bulbs. The compact fluorescents last ten times as long and save considerable energy. To illustrate this point, place your hand near one of each that have been lit for ten minutes. The heat you feel coming off of the incandescent bulb is wasted energy.

Another big energy waste is using an inappropriate amount of wattage for an area. Using the correct wattage will light the space with the correct amount of illumination for the activities in the space and save energy by not over lighting the space. In bathrooms, where you need to see details on a daily basis, use twenty-three watts. Secondary bathrooms require less light, so use nineteen watts. You will be able to see details, but it won't be as bright as the main bathrooms. In kitchens, install under counter task lighting and use nineteen watts or less. In living rooms you will need enough light to read or chat but it shouldn't be glaring; thirteen watts will do the trick. Bedroom reading and relaxing needs eleven watts.

Burned-out fluorescent lamps should always be disposed of properly, through facilities that capture the mercury and recycle the components. Don't throw them away in just any trashcan.

Every Ikea *(www.ikea.com)* has a recycling center in the customer service area. In addition to compact fluorescents, they take batteries, plastic and paper.

www.lamprecycle.org refers you to other sites with information about recycling centers in your area.

www.earth911.com locates recycling centers near you.

LED bulbs are the most efficient bulbs available today. They consume a fraction of the energy that incandescent bulbs do and because they are constantly evolving, the warm color is now very similar to that of incandescents. They do cost more, but last thirty times as long as incandescents,

creating a savings of $139 per bulb in utlity costs. The good news is that LEDs are continuously becoming more affordable and available in accessory fixtures.

Crane Company *(www.ccrane.com)* makes the Vivid series of bulbs and offers bulk discounts when you purchase for an entire home.

VENDORS

Stray Dog Designs *(www.Straydog-designs.com)* is an HGTV Greenhouse vendor with a collection of some of the most unique lamps I've ever seen. I'm talking shapes and colors nowhere else to be found. The products are handmade with recycled materials and local workers are paid fair wages. The company is a big supporter of local artisans, stray animals, and green social behavior. Every time you buy a Stray Dog Design product, they donate a portion of the profit to feed hungry children, shelter homeless families, and create loving homes for stray animals. This is one accessory you can own and feel really good about.

Kichler Lighting *(www.kichler.com)* carries an under cabinet LED puck light that works alone or in conjunction with the company's under cabinet LED strip.

Bruck *(www.brucklighting.com)* has expanded its green line to include the Kairos with Ledra. Its linear pendant has attractive fluorescent indirect uplighting and twenty-four watts of adjustable LED direct down lighting.

Rocky Mountain Hardware *(www.rockymountainhardware.com)* earns five gold stars from me. They are based in Idaho and they have a new line of LED indoor lighting that is gorgeous and made from 90 percent

Stray Dog Lamps simply has some of the most adorable accessory lamps available. I feel good knowing they are made from recyclable iron, like this Helen Johnston floor lamp and recycled cement bags like the papier-mache bird motif bedside lamp.

recycled metal. Using their light fixtures can help you to qualify for two points towards LEED certification. Their headquarters are LEED Gold certified.

LightGreen (*www.lightgreeninc.com*) specializes in stylish, modern, and energy-efficient fixtures using fluorescent, LED, and metal-halide technology. Cleaner, smaller, and simpler than ever before, these fixtures use less energy consumption and maintenance.

Touch (*www.do-not-touch.com*) sells eco-friendly lamps made of recycled materials. Creative designs, like lamps made from coffee spoons or milk boxes, transforms would be trash into beautiful creations.

Boyd Lighting (*www.boydlighting.com*) has started selling LED fixtures. Everything Boyd manufactures is gorgeous and these new fixtures are no exception. They powder coat the inside to gain additional reflectance. Their proprietary LED light package provides 50,000 hours of lamp life (ten years of normal use), a color that rivals incandescent bulbs, and energy efficiency of forty-three lumens per watt.

3Form (*www.3-form.com*) has launched a new lighting division, Light Art, which is as eco-friendly as their panels. The resin-based light products are made from 3Form's Varia Ecoresin products which contain 40 percent recycled content.

Leucos (*www.leucosusa.com*) wall and ceiling fixtures are sculptural and turn any space into an experience. I like this line because most of the fixtures are available in fluorescent light sources.

Hudson Furniture (*www.hudsonfurnitureinc.com*) features a unique line of lamps, chandeliers, and table lamps made from reclaimed woods, recycled metals, and nontoxic, hand rubbed oil finishes.

WAC Lighting (*www.waclighting.com*) has an affordable, spunky collection of decorative lighting which comes in a wide variety of LED and fluorescent fixtures.

Home Energy (*www.homeenergy.org*) converts watts and calculates savings between incandescent and fluorescent bulbs.

AUTOMATED LIGHTING SYSTEMS

Using dimmers, timers, and motion detectors in conjunction with artificial light sources reduces energy loads in the home. Dimmers should be installed in dining, bedroom, living room, and hallways. Sensors should be placed in bathrooms, pantries, closets, hallways, and exterior lights. Timers work well with exterior lighting. Whole house automated systems can combine all of these functions with a centralized controller which runs programmable zones. Syncing these systems with phone, Internet and security systems provides the most efficient energy use and eliminates waste.

Lutron Electronics (*www.lutron.com*) is a world leader in residential lighting control systems. The company offers a wide selection of light dimmers, entire home diming systems, and motorized window treatments.

Control4 (*www.Control4.com*) is an affordable, scalable system which operates efficiently and even alerts you via email in the event of a water leak, fire, or security breach. With access screens that can be viewed throughout the home or via the Internet, Control4 provides homeowners peace of mind while respecting the planet. Brochures are printed on recycled materials.

SOY VEGETABLE CANDLES VS. PETROLEUM PARAFFIN CANDLES

When you think of candlelight, relaxing, spa-like environments come to mind. Candlelight can be a soothing and wonderful way to create a mood, but most candles are toxic when they're burned, releasing harmful chemicals into the air. Most candles are also made from petroleum by-products and contain benzene and toluene. Both are known carcinogens. Artificially scented candles may contain phthalates. Once these paraffin candles are burned, they release these chemicals and add to indoor air pollution.

Soy or beeswax candles burn longer and cleaner. Soy wax spills are easier to clean compared to paraffin candle wax, which stains fabric and carpets. Soy candles also act as a diffuser because they burn slower, allowing for a cooler flame near the oil. When the oil is not burned, it diffuses around the room more evenly.

I just received a coffee-scented candle from Paradise Candles of Hawaii (*www.paradisecandlesofhawaii.com*) for my birthday. In addition to the amazing smell, the candle is made of high-quality soy wax and botanical oils. It comes from renewable resources supporting U.S. farmers, is biodegradable, contains no petroleum by-products, has 100 percent all natural wicks, and is hand crafted.

Bluecorn Naturals (*www.beeswaxcandles.com*) sells raw natural beeswax and soy candles and nontoxic candles in a wide selection of colors.

Lori Dennis (*www.loridennis.com*) features handmade, 100 percent pure beeswax, unbleached candles. The beeswax is made by local U.S. honeybees and contains no artificial fragrance. Wicks consist only of cotton, without any metal or lead. Long burning with a soft, honey smell, you will fall in love with these candles.

Anna Sova's (*www.annasova.com*) soy vegetable candles are a healthy mixture of soy and vegetable wax and are vegan friendly. The scents are created using essential oils for a long-lasting, all natural effect.

3 FABRICS AND WINDOW TREATMENTS

The choices in eco-friendly fabrics have really expanded in the last ten years. The variety of textures, patterns, and colors now rival that of mainstream fabrics due to advances in green manufacturing and raw material sourcing. But at a time when every company is calling their product eco-friendly or green, how can we make the best choices? There are degrees of how sustainable a fabric is and, in addition to your own research, labels and organizations like GOTS, Greenguard, and Green Seal can help you make that determination. Ask yourself the following questions below when researching fabric for your projects.

Is the fabric and its manufacturing process free of harmful chemicals? Any of 2,000 chemicals can be used during the manufacturing process, leaving residual amounts in the fabrics that can leach into the water supply, pollute the air, and be absorbed by our skin. Formaldehyde, for example, is frequently used in conventional manufacturing to help cloth retain its uniformity (won't bunch) and size (won't shrink). Not only is this process toxic to the environment and consumers but also to the employees who handle the chemical for forty hours every week. Organic fabric manufacturers are giving the consumer an option to purchase textiles without the chemical additives.

Is it from a renewable resource? If it's a synthetic fiber, is it 100 percent recyclable and made from recycled content material? Is it antique?

When the fiber comes from an animal has it been purchased from a farm that is free range and doesn't practice animal cruelty?

How long will the fabric be useable before it shows signs of wear and needs to be replaced? The more durable a fabric is, the longer it will last. Long-lasting fabric is more environmentally friendly than that which must be replaced often. Treatments like Nano-Tex, an environmentally friendly permanent stain repellent finish, make fabrics easy to clean and withstand years of use.

Is the fabric biodegradable? Is there an alternative option to becoming part of the waste stream at the end of its useful life? As a side note here, consider donating excess fabric or worn out fabric to design schools. They are in constant need of fabrics for projects. Imagine your old bedspread could be an inspiration in Armani's line one day. And you kept the fabric out of the trash.

Using antique fabrics is a yet another way to reduce your carbon footprint. Some of the loveliest antique fabrics you can find are at Nathan Turner's shop in Los Angeles. These throw pillows and susani are made from fabric that is over a hundred years old. In this Old World courtyard, they were the perfect finishing touch to soften the sea of stone.

Fabrics are made from plant fibers, animal fibers, and synthetic fibers. We've all seen the ad touting material as "all natural." While the word does have a wholesome ring to it, it certainly doesn't mean it's nontoxic, healthy, or a good choice. Reviewing where the fibers come from helps you to make informed decisions about the appropriate types of fabric to use in your interior or exterior spaces.

PLANT FIBERS
Cotton
When you see a label saying a fabric is "natural cotton" you may think it's a green choice. The truth is that conventional cotton, although a small percentage of the world's agricultural crops, uses 25 percent of the world's pesticides. Every pound of cotton that is grown uses a third of a pound of pesticide, which pollutes the groundwater in many countries. On the other hand, organic cotton is a green fiber. Never genetically modified, it doesn't use poisonous chemicals found in polluting pesticides, herbicides, and fertilizers. Instead, eco-friendly techniques like crop rotation and introduction of natural predators are used in organic cotton cultivation. All organic cotton farmers must meet GOTS standards during cultivation and production. Organic certification also includes annual inspections of land and crops by reputable certifying organizations.

Linen
Linen comes from the flax pant. Although growing flax creates far less pollution than cotton cultivation, the growing of flax requires mass quantities of herbicides, as flax is not competitive with weeds. The conventional growing of flax pollutes water through a process called "retting" which separates the fiber from the stalk by rotting it away. This process creates butyric acid, methane, and hydrogen sulfide which has a rotten smell. If the water is not treated before its disposal, it creates pollution in waterways. Organic flax cultivation requires manual weeding and rotation of crops to fight off weeds and potential disease. Organic producers of flax "artificially ret" the flax and this method results in no toxic wastewater. With its high moisture absorbency, high heat conductivity, and excellent abrasion resistance, linen (flax) is an excellent choice for upholstery.

Bamboo
Often called a sustainable wonder plant, bamboo is a renewable fiber that has natural antibacterial qualities. The plants grows quickly, doesn't require pesticides, absorbs four times the CO_2 that trees do, and releases 35 percent more oxygen.

Nettle

Nettle, a common weed, has been called the next bamboo. Plants grow quickly without the use of pesticides. They are mowed and dried once per year and require replanting only once every fifteen years. The fabric hasn't been marketed very well, but is a cost-competitive alternative to cotton.

Hemp

Hemp is an extremely durable fabric that naturally resists mold and UV light, and can be machine-washed. It's a great choice for a shower curtain, drapery, or slip-covered furniture. It grows fast in any kind of climate, uses little water, does not exhaust the soil, and requires no pesticides or herbicides. It is considered by many as the most versatile and sustainable plant on the earth because of its many uses: biofuels, paper, fabrics, ropes, building material, skin care products, and even food. And no, eating hemp will not get you high.

Seacell

Seacell fabric is man made cellulose fabric made out of wood pulp fiber (lyocell) and seaweed. The theory is that your skin will absorb the nutrients from seaweed (which combats cellulite), so bedding made of seacell fabric is a desirable, detoxing option.

Soy Fiber

Soy fiber is made from the waste product of soybeans. Organic cultivation does not require any bleach or toxins when soy is processed into fibers for fabric. Soy fiber fabric is called vegetarian cashmere because it is extremely soft. The fabric is resistant to UV rays and naturally anti-bacterial.

Lyocell

Lyocell is a fiber made from wood pulp cellulose. It is strong, soft, naturally wrinkle resistant, and absorbent. It drapes well which makes it an ideal choice for fabric drapery treatments.

Bark Cloth

Made from the bark of Mutuba trees, bark cloth is a 100 percent biodegradable, sustainable material. Textures range from fleece to leather-like, and it can be molded.

ANIMAL FIBERS

Wool

Made from sheep hair, wool is renewable, biodegradable, and durable, yet soft. The fabric is wrinkle resistant and retains shape well. Wool has natural insulative properties, which makes it good for bedding and drapery.

Cashmere

Cashmere comes from the hair of Kashmir goats. The hair is collected every spring and hand woven into a fine, soft fabric. Because the fiber is so delicate, resulting in the need to handle collection, manufacturing, and processing by hand, cashmere is a sustainable and energy efficient fabric.

Alpaca

Alpaca fiber is considered one of the best fabrics because it is as soft as cashmere, warmer than wool, more durable than cotton, and is naturally hypoallergenic due to the absence of lanolin. The material does not mat or pill and is naturally stain and wrinkle resistant. The material is so strong that 3,000 year old, intact pieces have been found in the Peruvian mountains.

Camel Hair

Also called camel wool, this fabric has similar characteristics to wool and cashmere. It is collected as camels naturally shed in the late spring. The fabric has a rich, well, camel color, which doesn't need to be dyed. Its adaptable humidity qualities that change with moisture air content make it perfect for bedding and upholstery. It also becomes softer every time it is washed.

Leather

Organic leather sounds like an oxymoron. However, the leather used is actually a byproduct of cows that were raised for their meat. The hides come from animals that are organically fed and humanely treated. The conventional technique used to tan leather involves chrome and other heavy metals that emit toxic fumes and contaminate water and air. During an organic tanning process natural plant matter is used to cure the leather rather than toxic chemicals.

Silk

Silk comes from the unwound fiber of silkworm cocoons. It is a renewable, biodegradable, durable fabric. Conventional silk kills the moth by steaming it to death so it can obtain an intact cocoon with longer fibers. Organic silk farming allows the moth to leave the cocoon and then collects them for processing. This method results in much shorter fibers (that the moth has broken through) resulting in lower yield and higher-priced silk.

SYNTHETIC FABRICS

Although many synthetic fabrics are made from petroleum-based products, they can still be considered green. Some synthetic fabrics are spun from recycled pre- and post-consumer materials, like plastic bottles and waste from industrial production. This diverts waste from landfills

Living room by Lori Dennis, photo by Ken Hayden

and converts it into useful raw materials. Some of these recycled content fabrics are extremely durable and last many lifetimes. Even more sustainable are fabrics created from recycled waste, which can be recycled into new raw materials when their lifespan is over. In the recent past synthetic fabrics used in contract applications looked commercial. Innovations in technology and boutique hotel popularity, however, have transformed the look of these fabrics into suitable styles for residential interiors. These types of synthetics are easily cleaned, fire resistant, contain recycled and recyclable content, and look fabulous.

The factories that manufacture these eco-friendly materials practice environmental responsibility in their factories and when shipping. Many follow strict GOTS guidelines, use low impact ink, recycle waste into usable materials, test for indoor air quality, follow fair trade standards and pay living wages.

VENDORS

Hemp Traders (*www.hemptraders.com*) specializes in hemp fabrics that have not been treated with chemicals. They carry a wide variety of textures and patterns.

EnviroTextiles (*www.envirotextile.com*) carries hemp and cotton products and provides free sample kits.

Bark Cloth (*www.barkcloth.de*) sells cloth made of the bark from eco-certified Mutuba tree farms in Uganda.

Tenbro (*www.tenbro.com*) is a wholesaler of bamboo fabric in a wide array of colors and patterns.

Lynn Caldwell (*www.lcweave.com*) sells bamboo fabric in artisan colors and weaves.

Harts Fabric (*www.hartsfabric.com*) carries an affordable line of organic cotton, hemp, bamboo, eco felt, ramie, seacell, and natural dye fabrics and organic batting.

Pick Natural (*www.picknatural.com*) features eco-friendly fabrics in hemp, organic linen, organic cotton, bamboo, soy, silk, wool, yak down, and lyocell in a variety of colors, textures, and patterns.

EcoHides (*www.ecohides.com*) sells earth-friendly, high-quality leather tanned with natural vegetable products and waxes.

Mike Ragan Rags (*www.usarags.com*) offers a wide

Living room by Lori Dennis, photo by Christian Romero

Sensuede is a synthetic fiber made of recycled materials. I love using it when I upholster in light colors because it's easy to keep clean. No need to panic when dirty hands touch this sofa; you simply spot clean with a cotton towel soaked in mild dish soap and water. Voila, the light-colored sofa is as good as new.

selection of eco-friendly fabrics ranging from cottons to micro fibers to faux crocodile and is simply the nicest vendor you will ever know.

Spoonflower (*www.spoonflower.com*) allows you design and print your own patterns on GOTS certified organic cotton and bamboo fabrics.

Shumacher Terra (*www.fschumacher.com*) is a new brand of fabrics made from 100 percent USDA organic certified cotton. A portion of the proceeds supports Water Aid America, which provides clean water to communities in need around the globe. They also sell products made from 100 percent recycled polyester. Specific fabrics, designated by a Green Leaf logo, meet Oeko-Tex Standard 100 and ISO certifications for safe dyeing, bleaching and finishing processes, as well as for social responsibility.

S. Harris (*www.sharris.com*) has a Cradle to Cradle certification on its Fern Tree fabric. The fabric is partly woven from recycled plastic bags and is completely recyclable when its lifespan is over.

Robert Allen (*www.robertallendesign.com*) just launched an entirely green fabric line called Awakenings. They use low-impact dyes and organic cottons to meet and exceed Global Organic Textile Standards.

Designtex (*www.designtex.com*) has always been known for their modern styled, colorful fabrics. They can now offer a woven made of Trevira CS, a low impact, recyclable polyester that is Cradle to Cradle certified.

Pollack (*www.pollackassociates.com*) is one of my favorite manufacturers. You can see plenty of their products in my designs. Every collection offers more eco-friendly choices made from recycled content and renewable plant sources.

Harmony Art (*www.harmonyart.com*) has some very inexpensive, double wide, biodegradable organic textiles. The designs are pretty trippy, but I'm into that. They're also GOTS compliant.

NearSea Naturals (*www.nearseanaturals.com*), located in an off-grid, solar-powered facility in New Mexico, offers organic cotton, wool, and hemp from organic or sustainable sources. Their eco-friendly fabrics are sold by the yard or roll, and they carry batting, stuffing, bias, twill tapes, and button made of recycled materials.

Maharam (*www.maharam.com*) has one of the coolest, user-friendly Web sites I've ever seen for a fabric vendor. The selection of green fabrics is unusual and will make any room sing. They are Greenguard certified for their support of reduced emissions and do not use heavy metal dyes.

Twill Textiles (*www.twilltextiles.com*) offer some great fabrics with a menswear look made of organic wool-ramie blend. They are biodegradable and Cradle to Cradle certified. Any scrap that is not turned into felt for non-woven upholstery is transformed into gardening mulch.

O Ecotextiles (*www.oecotextiles.com*) uses only sustainably grown fibers and has an independent Indoor Air Quality lab test for chemical emissions. Among some of the most luxurious fabrics in the world, the lines include Belgian linen spun into yarn by a master and long fiber hemp retted by craftsmen who practice ancient traditions. All O Ecotextiles can be used for LEED indoor air quality points.

Kravet (*www.kravet.com*) carries a recycled polyester made from consumer waste like plastic bottles. Although their fabrics look very sophisticated, this line is nearly indestructible. The factory follows strict GOTS guidelines, uses low impact ink, and has a special process of dyeing the warps that reduces yarn waste.

Architex (*www.architex-ljh.com*) carries the Angela Adams green collection, which incorporates geometric and nature inspired patterns made from pre-consumer polyester recycled fibers and has achieved Cradle to Cradle Silver Certification.

Edelman Leather (*www.edelmanleather.com*) is 100 percent Greenguard certified—a faux line of leathers

From drapery to bedding to furniture, fabric makes up a huge part of our interior design budgets. Thankfully eco friendly choices are becoming abundant and are some of the finest looking sold today. Innovators like Brentano, Calvin, Creation Bauman, Pollack, and Thomas Lavin are bringing fresh, fabulous fabrics to market while keeping in mind our health and the environment.

Pollack Cameo 2330-06

Creation Baumann Valentino 414

Calvin Graphite 10912

Bretano City Block 3925-09

which are antimicrobial, antifungal and antibacterial.

Thomas Lavin (*www.thomaslavin.com*) is a world-renowned stylemaker and everything in his shop is divine. Creation Bauman is one of his newer eco-friendly lines. This 100-year-old company began sustainable manufacturing in 1973 and takes measures to ensure that the manufacturing, production, shipping, and packaging of their fabrics is environmentally responsible.

The Pindler Green line (*www.pindler.com*) meets third party certification and all fabrics are free of heavy metals and chemical dyes. The manufacturing process includes sustainable behaviors like the use of wind power. The line includes organic and sustainable fabrics such as flax, organic cotton, wool, hemp, silk, linen, and jute. Recently they've introduced a line made of 100 percent recycled polyester, commonly sourced from plastic (PET) bottles.

Jason Asch of Diamond Fabric (*www.diamondfoamandfabric.com*) is one of the most knowledgeable people I ever talked to about fabrics and, for that matter, a lot of other organic subjects. He stocks a large collection of certified organic fabrics but also stocks plenty of European fabrics that have been manufacturing organically for years without ever certifying. One rep told him that waste water from his factory is so clean that he and his sons fish for lunch in the very same river where the factory empties its waste water.

Calvin Belgian Hopsack linen (*www.calvinfabrics.com*) is a fine solution to your neutral, solid needs. It isn't dyed or bleached and is finished with an organic enzyme that leaves no chemical residue.

Sina Pearson Textiles' (*www.sinapearson.com*) elegant and sophisticated line includes Cradle to Cradle gold and Greenguard certifications.

Mod Green Pod (*www.modgreenpod.com*) is a member of the Organic Trade Association that follows the GOTS protocol and offers bold, whimsical, printed patterns on organic cotton

Silver State (*www.silverstatefabrics.com*) sells the Body and Soul and Winds of Change collections, both made of 100 percent recycled and recyclable material and can contribute to LEED credits.

Rubie Green's (*www.rubiegreen.com*) flirtatious, organic cotton prints are a breath of fresh air, and I love that this GOTS certified company gives instructions on how to launder their products in an eco-friendly manner.

Sensuede (*www.sensuede.com*) is the first luxury faux suede fabric that's eco-friendly. Made entirely from recycled plastic bottles and polyester fibers, Sensuede is durable and luxurious. The Silky and Flannel Suede lines come in a wide variety of colors.

Carnegie Fabrics' (*www.carnegiefabrics.com*)

Indoor and outdoor living can be an organic experience in more ways than one. Durable Sunbrella fabric and Anna Sova organic towels make a splash at this poolside exterior. Sunbrella (*www.sunbrella.com*) makes some of my favorite fabrics. I've used them for awnings, outdoor drapery, outdoor throws, and all types of upholstery. The company offers recycling for its customers using pre- and post-consumer waste and repurposing it into a variety of recycled products. During manufacturing the company dramatically reduces water and energy consumption and avoids harmful effluents in the dyeing process. Sunbrella is Greenguard certified for indoor air quality. Awnings are a large part of Sunbrella's business and by virtue of their design intent of reducing solar rays' intrusion into buildings, they help to eliminate 10 to 40 percent of cooling needs.

Xorel line has an extensive collection of bold graphic fabrics with Cradle to Cradle rating.

Several of Fabricut's Environment Plus fabrics (*www.fabricut.com*) contain 100 percent recycled content and meet strict Oeko-Tex Standard 100 and Cradle to Cradle certification.

OUTDOOR

Outdoor fabrics have come such a long way in terms of aesthetics. Now many of them are even more beautiful than indoor fabrics. Whenever possible I try to use them for upholstery because they are ultra durable and very resistant to fading, wear, and tear. Many of these fabrics can be cleaned in a washing machine, so there is no need for dry cleaning. It also makes your decorating transition from indoor to outdoor rooms seamless. Many outdoor fabrics come in luxurious velvets and sheers with coordinating tassels and trim.

Phifer's 100 percent Marquesa Furniture Fabric (*www.phifer.com*) is a one hundred percent recyclable, PVC-free fabric made from post-industrial waste by product. The fabric is highly durable, antimicrobial, stain resistant, fade resistant, easy to clean, and quick to dry.

Creation Baumann Lup 6

Creation Baumann Ossa 323

Thomas Lavin CB Flippa 199

Pollack Lodge 3018-02

Exterior by Lori Dennis, photo by Christian Romero

STAIN GUARDS

Prolonging fabric life by reducing the amount of stains and fading that may occur is a green practice, but many stain guards on the market are highly toxic. You can smell the VOC offgassing for months. While it is a good idea to extend the life of fabric by protecting it with a stain guard, it is imperative to select a nontoxic, environmentally friendly solution.

Ultra-Guard (*www.ultra-guard.com*) is nontoxic and hypoallergenic. It repels both oil- and water-based stains and contains ultraviolet inhibitors to reduce fading.

303 Fabric Guard (*www.sailrite.com*) is endorsed by Sunbrella for protection against mildew-, oil-, and water-based stains and fading from the sun. The product is non-toxic and odorless when it dries.

WINDOW TREATMENTS

Window treatments are green by design—they are intended to help to control the amount of heat gain or loss through windows. Their insulating and light blocking properties help to reduce heating and cooling energy loads. Their materials should consist of renewable, nontoxic fibers which do not emit harmful VOCs. Some imported plastic or PVC blinds have been found to break down in ultraviolet light and produce toxic dust and have been known to offgas for their entire lifespan. They should not be specified in a green home.

Window treatments must be cleverly designed to be able to utilize the natural power of solar energy to light a room, but strong enough to withstand its deteriorating effects. Successful designs will allow natural light in interiors while still providing privacy.

When an occupant in the home is an allergy or asthma sufferer, blinds, which can be regularly vacuumed, are a better choice than fabric treatments. If you customize window treatments with a local fabricator, be sure to supply them with or specify sustainable fabric.

Fabric Window Treatments

Anna Sova (*www.annasova.com*) offers finished panels in 100 percent eco silk and organic cotton. The silk does not contain any rayon or polyester fillers and has no toxic residues from finishing. No Anna Sova products use dioxins, bleach, heavy metal dyes, or toxic finishing.

Lutron (*www.lutron.com*) offers automated roller shades, drapery track systems, and skylight shades available in a variety of fabrics and can sync with a whole house light control system.

Eco Terric (*www.eco-terric.com*) offers organic drapery panels produced in India under strict Fair Trade principles and fabric window shades made without chemicals or harsh dyes.

Library by Lori Dennis, photo by Mark Tanner

Closing the curtains can save an average of 25 percent on heat in the winter and air conditioning in the summer. Make your carbon footprint even lighter by using an organic fabric like the one shown in this library. When privacy is needed, but you want to take advantage of natural light, consider a sheer top and opaque bottom, as shown in this eco-friendly loft.

Cozy Curtains (*www.cozycurtains.com*) sells the Warm Window system, a unique Roman shade system constructed of four layer, insulated fabric with magnetic sealing edges to control drafts, radiation, and noise.

Rawganique (*www.rawganique.com*) carries hemp and linen window treatments in Roman shade and panel configurations. They come in various sizes and are chemical free, simple, and very elegant.

Eco Veil Mecho Shade System (*www.mechoshade.com*) is Cradle to Cradle certified, 100 percent recyclable, and available in a wide range of colors and density. I love these shades in any style because they can stand alone in a modern interior or hide behind a drapery treatment in a more traditional space. They help to keep the sun's heat from coming in and fading furniture and floors while still allowing a view. Mecho Shades also has the Solar Trac system, which automatically adjusts the position of the shades incrementally on the window to maximize view and daylight while protecting people and furnishings from direct sun and excessive glare.

Antique Drapery Rod (*www.antiquedraperyrod.com*) features metal hardware made from recycled, post-consumer content and can be recycled at the end of its useful life.

Natural Grass Shades

Besides being renewable resources which may only take a few months to replenish themselves, natural fibers in window shades have other advantages. They are appropriate for any style interior. Plants such as flax and hemp are durable and have a high resistance to ultraviolet rays. Many natural fibers, like bamboo, have antimicrobial properties that make them extremely resistant to mold. Some fibers, like flax, have a natural wax that makes a beautiful sheen on the window treatment material.

Living room by Lori Dennis, photo by Ken Hayden

Conrad Shades (*www.conradshades.com*) has, for the last fifty years, been a pioneer in sustainably designed, handwoven custom shades from renewable fibers. All materials used in their line of over eighty different shades are sustainably grown and harvested. Because the shades are hand made on looms, very little energy is used to produce them. Their durable products do not contain harmful toxins or VOCs. They employ a cottage industry of farmers and local artisans.

Earth Shade products (*www.earthshade.com*) are available in ten styles and all their patterns have insulating and sun shading properties. For colder climates they offer a hemp insulation liner. No pesticides are used in their crops and coloration is achieved by natural techniques like sun bleaching or oven baking. All shades are available in custom sizes, with optional automation systems and lifetime warranties.

Wood Blinds

Wood blinds can be a desirable choice for a green interior because they are easy to clean, long lasting, and do a good job of blocking out ultraviolet rays. Make sure they made of are FSC certified, composite, or faux wood.

The Shutter Store (*www.theshutterstore.com*) is one of the only FSC certified shutter companies in America. They sell affordable, custom sizes and distribute Kelly Hoppen's designer shutter line.

Wood Blinds and Shutter Factory (*www.wbsfactory.com*) has a wide variety of styles including blinds made of composite and faux wood, and shades made with 100 percent recyclable and renewable materials.

4 SURFACE MATERIALS

Now, unlike a decade ago, sustainable surface materials are easily found and come in a wide variety of attractive styles. Most of the time the price is right in line with conventional materials and the look is indistinguishable. Selecting sustainable products, however, makes a vast improvement in the effects these products have on environmental and human health. The reduction or elimination of pollutants significantly improves air quality for both indoor and outdoor environments. This is especially important for people who suffer the side effects of Sick Building Syndrome. Conservation of energy also reduces global warming and acid rain, greatly improving our planet's ability to sustain life. Using green materials aids in water conservation and waste reduction, and reuse and recycling materials helps to preserve precious natural resources. But in order for recycling to make economic sense, consumers will need to purchase materials made with recycled content. Purchasing surface materials made of recycled materials helps to fuel this need. Equally important, buying green materials ensures that laborers are not exposed to toxins and exploitation. It certainly feels right to know that the people who produce the materials that make our interiors shine are not being treated unfairly.

When selecting materials, it is also important to keep their future maintenance requirements in mind. For example, choosing smooth surface materials will make them easier to clean than textured ones, thereby using less time, energy, and cleaning products. This is especially true of bathroom and kitchen walls, which tend to get dirtier than any other walls in the home. Having washable surfaces like tile or semi-gloss paint helps to prevent stains and extends the life of these areas.

FLOORING
Wood Flooring

Wood is one of the most durable flooring materials. Often a wood floor that looks like it's past its prime simply

> Flooring choices heavily impact your design direction. Whether you are going for casual, beachy chic or a sophisticated Zen vibe, you can incorporate a sustainable floor material. In this entry, hand-scooped bamboo planks were impregnated with an espresso color that will hold up to busy foot traffic. Bamboo is a grass that regrows to full maturity much quicker than hard wood. It's generally pretty inexpensive too.

Kitchen by Lori Dennis, photo by Roi Yerushalmi

The kitchen in this Southern California beach house is exposed to sand, sea air (i.e. salt), and lots of guests who want to enjoy the Pacific Ocean. It was mandatory to have a low-maintenance, highly durable floor surface in the home. Our solution was to use reclaimed bleacher planks from a nearby high school. The homeowners and many of their guests actually sat on these very same bleachers when attending high school basketball games. It makes for a fun story and a floor that has clearly proven it can stand the test of time.

needs to be refinished. Consider this possibility before rushing out to buy something new or reclaimed. Once floors are refurbished, they may be more beautiful and durable than anything you can purchase. If you decide to take this route, seal the rest of the house off from the area that is being refinished so wood dust particles, which likely contain toxins, are not spread throughout the home. Depending on how old the floors are there may well be lead paint and other highly toxic substances that will be kicked up into the air and can make a homeowner extremely sick. Use low-VOC, water-based products for the new applications.

If a new or reclaimed wood floor is going to be installed, start with a green subfloor and products that have been FSC certified and contain no formaldehyde. They will emit lower levels of unhealthy chemicals. (Nontoxic subflooring is not always easy to locate and can be substantially higher-priced than conventional subfloor materials.)

Hardwood floors are so durable that they can sometimes last longer than their original homes. Older wood

Entry by Lori Dennis, photo by Ken Hayden

floors are often high-quality and beautiful. Because buildings use an extraordinary amount of new lumber, some green lumber companies specialize in finding reclaimed or used wood. Reusing old wood is a good green approach to reducing the amount of new lumber needed in a home. When using reclaimed lumber, make sure to instruct your installer to finish the reclaimed wood with environmentally friendly stains and finishes.

As a last resort, select new lumber for wood flooring. When doing so, it is imperative that the wood be from managed forests and be FSC certified.

Since 1992 Eco Timber (*www.ecotimber.com*) has been promoting forest conservation by selling sustainably harvested and reclaimed wood. The company offers exotic woods and bamboo and its forestry practices guarantee a continuous yield of high-quality timber while maintaining a healthy, regenerative forest ecosystem.

Elmwood Reclaimed Timber (*www.elmwoodreclaimedtimber.com*) is a green company with a great sense of humor. The catalog is actually fun to read. They specialize in reclaimed wood and have some of the most beautiful products I've seen. They give a portion of profits to a long list of environmental and social charities.

TerraMai (*www.terramai.com*) offers reclaimed hardwood from around the world. All of their wood is FSC certified. Former ski bums and river guides had the goal of saving forests and providing work for locals; sixteen years later they are a worldwide leader in sustainable materials. In one of my projects, TerraMai was able to supply me with wood flooring that had a previous life as bleachers at a local high school. This floor makes everyone smile when they hear of its origin.

(see chapter 9, Green Building, for more wood flooring sources)

Rapidly Renewable Flooring

Plant fibers such as bamboo, cork, and linoleum are fast growing, renewable materials that make unique and environmentally sound statements when installed as flooring.

Bamboo grows quickly and is extremely hard. It takes four to seven years to regenerate, making it a better choice than oak or pine which each take about twenty years. Bamboo comes in a very wide selection of colors and styles, and is generally much less expensive than FSC-certified hardwood. In one of my projects I installed hand scooped bamboo that looked like an exotic hardwood; people are constantly surprised to learn it is really bamboo. Typically bamboo is glued, not nailed down, so be sure to specify a nontoxic glue.

Cork is made from bark that has been peeled from Spanish Oaks. Because it provides a cushioning under feet and absorbs sound, kitchens and home spas are a great place to install this material. It is also a great insulator, hygienic, antiallergenic, water resistant, does not trap dirt or fungus, and is easy to maintain. I always had a hard time installing cork for flooring because I felt that it resembled a '70s family room. Although I loved the way cork can look on a wall, I was not a huge fan of cork on the floor. Recently, however, I saw a house with cork mosaic on the floor of the wine cellar. People were bending down to touch it because no one knew what it was, even me. Anytime people want to touch a material you've installed, I call it a success. This particular product looks like ceramic penny tiles but is actually slices of used wine stoppers. Once it's grouted and sealed, it's completely waterproof. It totally changed my mind about cork flooring.

Linoleum is made the same way it has been for decades, manufactured from linseed oil, sawdust, cork, and pigments all mixed together and backed by jute fiber. It is extremely resistant to fire and does not melt. Durable linoleum flooring can last for thirty to forty years. When its lifecycle comes to an end, linoleum is biodegradable and can be composted.

Recycled rubber floors are an excellent choice if you are designing spaces for young children, basements, yoga studios, or a home gym. Tiles made from recycled rubber tires are safe, antimicrobial, waterproof, can be nontoxic and have very good sound and temperature insulation. Rubber tiles come in many colors and textures and are extremely easy to install.

Lumber Liquidators (*www.lumberliquidators.com*) carries a good selection of bamboo that is easy to install. They warranty their floors for twenty-five years.

Duro Design (*www.durodesign.com*) sells cork, bamboo, eucalyptus, and FSC hardwood flooring. They create stylish, easy-to-maintain flooring, which is vibrant in color. They have a state of the art, low VOC, water-based dyeing system that is non-yellowing, thick, flexible, and extremely durable. They will work with designers on custom color floors.

Jelinek Cork Group (*www.jelinek.com*) is a 150-year-old cork company that not only started a recycling program for cork wine stoppers, but also gives a portion of the proceeds to environmental and social charities. They sell the mosaic cork flooring made from wine stoppers I mentioned.

The Cork Store (*www.corkstore.com*) sells all things cork, from flooring to furniture, and all at factory outlet prices.

Floor Score (*www.floorscore.com*) sells about ten different styles of rubber flooring tiles. They are made from recycled tires, come in a wide selection of colors, and are all easy to install.

Forbo (*www.forbo.com*) sells linoleum under the

Marmoleum brand name. They are an environmentally transparent company that publishes its product Life Cycle Assessment showing products' environmental impact throughout their life cycles. They use 45 percent post-industrial recycled content in their products, run their plants on renewable energy, like wind power, and recycle 100 percent of their factory scrap back into the process. Their Field to Field program works with farmers who use proper crop rotation and no till methods. They encourage designers to return unused samples in self-addressed stamped envelopes and then resend those same samples out to other customers.

Hard Surface Flooring

Concrete, terrazzo, natural stone, and ceramic tile are the longest lasting of floor materials. I've visited centuries-old ruins on the shores of the Mediterranean Sea and seen mosaic stone and cement floors that are still intact. You will be hard pressed to find flooring materials more durable than these. They also have beneficial health properties because they do not emit fibers, gases, or harmful byproducts. They do not absorb smoke, fumes, or contaminants.

Refinishing a concrete floor is the best green choice of the hard surface flooring materials because the least amount of material must be applied. Old slabs can be given a gorgeous new life given the advances in grinding, hardening, coloring, and polishing technologies. New concrete floors are also a good choice if you specify a cement with fly ash content. Fly ash is a recycled by product of power plants and reduces the amount of portand cement (a labor intensive material) that must be used. A new cement floor does not require a subfloor, so again, fewer materials and energy are needed.

Tile and terrazzo floors are easy to clean and can be made from pre- and post-consumer recycled content. The installers should be instructed to use low toxic grouts, sealers and glues. The bigger the tiles, the less grout you will need. Less grout means less possibility of mold buildup and, consequently, less cleaning.

Ceramic tile also has the benefit of being able to achieve the look of wood or natural stone without ever having to refinish or seal the tile. Additionally, individual damaged tiles can easily be replaced instead of entire sections of materials. Ceramic tile doesn't fade or discolor when exposed to UV rays. It can even withstand fire or floods.

Natural stone floors will last many lifetimes, but may often require routine sealer applications as part of their maintenance. Choose eco-friendly sealers, glues, and grouts. If possible, specify a stone that is located in your region (within a 500-mile radius). Most likely it will be less expensive and reduce the pollution that is created

When people ask me what is more durable, porcelain tile or natural stone, I always think about these images from Caesarea in Israel. There are parts of these ancient floors that look like they were installed last week even though they've been exposed to sun, sand, and salt water for about two thousand years. I can't deny that porcelain is a heavy-duty material that is often appropriate for the harshest of commercial interiors, but natural stone obviously can hold its own.

when a large amount of a heavy, foreign stone is delivered. Or specify from well-managed quarries.

In the factory and office, Trend (*www.trending-green.com*) practices eco awareness by using certified ecological paper to print all advertising materials (or those which haven't yet been digitized). Terrazzo is rarely seen in residential installations because of the cost and labor involved in pouring terrazzo. Trend has a 1/4" thick tile that is made from 72 percent recycled glass from wine, liquor, and water bottles mixed with resin. Since they are nearly 1/4" less thick than most terrazzo tiles they are much easier to work with, including custom cuts and installing right over existing floors.

Sandhill Industries (*www.sandhillind.com*) manufactures floor and wall tiles from 100 percent recycled glass. Recycled glass tiles take one half of the energy it takes to make ceramic tiles and keeps glass out of landfills. Tiles are available in thirty-six colors and a wide variety of shapes and sizes. Made in Idaho, USA, this company has received an EPA Evergreen Award for environmental practices as a manufacturer.

Country Floors (*www.countryfloors.com*) provides an extensive selection of in-stock reclaimed terracotta and LEED-certified porcelain.

(see "Tile" in the "Walls and Ceilings" section of this chapter for more vendors)

Carpet

Recently I was blasted on a carpeting blog for publicly stating that, "as a rule my firm does not specify wall-to-wall carpeting." Since the blogger is in the business of selling wall-to-wall carpeting, he didn't like the idea that I, or any designer, would make such a comment. The reasons I take a stance against wall-to-wall carpet is for the environment and human health. Most inexpensive carpets are made from nylon olefin which are toxic petrochemicals derived from petroleum. These carpets contain formaldehyde, toluene, and xylene, which are all toxic to the nervous system. They offgas these fumes for many years—sometimes throughout their entire lifespan. When they are disposed, most of them wind up in landfills and leach poisonous chemicals into the earth. About 3.5 billion tons of used, toxic wall-to-wall carpeting and padding winds up in landfills every year. So, if you're going to use wall–to-wall carpeting, make sure to ask about the company's recycling program. The easiest to recycle is carpet made of natural fibers because it can be composted or used as a layer of mulch underneath wood bark or gravel to reduce weeds.

What about wool? Wool doesn't offgas toxins, so it is a better environmental choice than synthetic carpet. But the problem, in addition to being cost prohibitive for most budgets, is that the backing of the carpet is loaded with highly reactive compounds and noxious glues. The padding is generally made of urethane and foamed with hydrocarbons such as methyl or bonded urethanes. These products contribute to Sick Building Syndrome and all of the symptoms that come with it. Avoid any carpet or pad that contains harmful chemicals, like stain protectors and other finishes. Check for Greenguard and Green Label certification.

Also problematic is since wall-to-wall carpets are fixed to the floor, they can never really be cleaned thoroughly. You can vacuum multiple times, everyday, with the best vacuums available and you will never be able to get all of the dust, dirt, and microorganisms that are embedded in the three layers of carpet, backing, and padding. This practically untreatable condition is the perfect environment for mold and fungus to grow, even if there is not a lot of moisture in the room. The reality is that liquids are often spilled on carpets and if they're not completely dry in a twenty-four hour period, mold will most likely occur.

If you're involved in a remodel and have to remove wall-to-wall carpeting, cross your fingers—you could have a gorgeous wood, tile, or cement floor under the old carpet.

For people who just won't live without carpets, I suggest large area rugs made of natural or recyclable fibers. Natural carpet materials include: wool, cotton, bamboo, jute, or hemp. When they are placed on hard surfaces, large rugs have the same benefits of softening an area, but they can also be removed for cleaning the rugs and the floor beneath them. Carpet tiles made of recycled and refurbished carpets are another option. If moisture, stains, or wear occurs, you simply replace the individual carpet tile. These tiles do not emit fumes, which also makes them a greener choice.

Pottery Barn (*www.potterybarn.com*) has a rug pad made of 100 percent recycled fibers. It's easily trimmed with household scissors to fit any rug.

Green Floors (*www.greenfloors.com*) is a major source of environmentally friendly flooring products. In addition to nontoxic carpets, carpet tiles, and rug pads, they sell a long list of green flooring materials. They also have a carpet recycling program to help reduce the billions of tons of synthetic carpets that retire in landfills each year.

Helios Carpet (*www.helioscarpet.com*) sells extremely stylish, upscale wool carpets. They can be installed as area rugs or as wall-to-wall. The wool, which is biodegradable and sustainable, comes from New Zealand sheep raised in open, clean, and sustainable pastures. Helios carpets are woven, not tufted which increases their longevity by 200 percent. The site includes a personal carbon footprint test and makes suggestions on how to reduce it.

Flor (*www.flor.com*) makes carpet tile from renewable and recyclable tile. The company has an easy return and recycle program for worn or damaged tiles. The company catalog is printed on recycled paper and their plants are energy efficient, using renewable sources for power. All

I'm a big fan of carpets made from renewable materials. They tend to be inexpensive, look amazing, and add interesting texture to interior spaces. The Natural Carpet Company, in Los Angeles, has a superior selection of area rugs that meet all of these criteria.

tiles are manufactured in the United States and are shipped in a condensed, flat pack, which can be used to send old tile back to them. They are members of Mission Zero, a nonprofit organization working toward zero environmental impact. Interface, Flor's parent company, has named 2020 the year they hope to achieve this goal.

Bentley Prince Street (*www.bentleyprincestreet.com*) offers hip patterned, recycled content carpet and a promise to reclaim all of their products to guarantee that they will not end up in a landfill. The company has been voted as one of the best places to work in Los Angeles, they are a Mission Zero member, and donate time and resources to many social and environmental charities.

All rugs featured by the Rug Company (*www.therug-company.com*) are handmade and designed by the world's most distinguished and experienced designers ensuring that their rugs will become heirlooms to be passed down from generation to generation.

Milliken (*www.millikencontract.com*) is the only textile manufacturer that has achieved carbon negative status. That means that they capture and offset more carbon dioxide than they emit, in their case 10 percent more. The company uses their own hydroelectric power, harvests 80 percent of the methane from a local landfill, and uses waste water treatment biosolids as a fuel source. Twenty years ago they removed all PVC from their products and currently every Milliken product has a Green Label Plus certification. Since 1999 they have sent zero waste to landfills. All their carpets are renewed, reused and recycled. When Milliken carpet replaces an old carpet (theirs or not) they choose the highest form of recovery possible. They also participate in sample return program for designers.

West Elm (*www.westelm.com*) has some of the most affordable and attractive natural, renewable resource fiber carpets I've found, and trust me, I've looked and looked and looked. Even though West Elm generally has a modern aesthetic, their natural fiber collection is versatile enough to fit in traditional to contemporary interiors.

Sunbrella (*www.sunbrella.com*), known worldwide for their superior outdoor fabrics, also makes rugs. They hold up against the elements and are easily cleaned with soap and water. Their rugs can be used indoors or outside. The company offers a recycling program and uses reclaimed materials for a variety of products.

Gaiam (*www.gaiam.com*) sells outdoor rugs in funky, Asian-inspired patterns made from 100 percent recycled plastic.

WALLS AND CEILINGS

The surfaces of walls and ceilings can be covered in paint, wallpaper, stone, tile, plaster, and paneling. The square footage of surface materials used on walls is more than any other surface in the home, creating potential health hazards if nontoxic products are not specified. Because walls are such a large part of any home, you have an extraordinary opportunity to make a design statement using a large portion of green materials that are healthy for the planet and the people occupying the space.

Paint

Primarily because paint is the least expensive product and has the least expensive application process for interior walls, a lot of it is used in residential homes. But when it comes to poor indoor air quality, paint is a major culprit. If you do not specify an eco-friendly paint, you are subjecting the occupants to volatile organic compounds (that "new" paint smell), carcinogens that can cause kidney damage, headaches, loss of muscle control, dizziness, and irregular heartbeats. Until recently it was difficult to find synthetic, no or low VOC paint in a wide variety of colors. Now many companies offer thousands of colors in formulas that contain no VOCs. However, no VOC doesn't mean the paint is entirely nontoxic. Most interior no or low VOC paints contain components that are derived from petroleum products. Check with the manufacturer that the paint you are using is water-based. Water-based acrylics are less toxic, more affordable, and extremely durable. Greenseal or Greenguard can help you determine how green your paint is.

For people who are sensitive to the chemicals in low or no VOC paints, some manufacturers are producing natural paints, made from plant oils and minerals. I've come across a few manufacturers who claim their paint is so safe that you can eat it without getting sick.

Be sure to specify the appropriate sheen for each room. For instance, high-humidity rooms like kitchens and bathrooms need a high-sheen, durable paint because they are washed more frequently. Using lighter colors will help to distribute daylight deeper into the home.

If you have leftover paint at the end of the project, don't dump wet paint into the trash or down a drain. If you must dispose of it, let it dry completely (latex paint is not hazardous once it has dried). Better, donate unused low or no VOC paint to a women's/children's shelter. If it's sealed properly, it will last a very long time. Many times volunteers or the occupants will donate time to make improvements, but lack the materials. Something as simple as the paint you no longer need can brighten a child's world.

Anna Sova (*www.annasova.com*) produces paint with up to 90 percent food ingredients. Their paint does not contain toxic chemicals like crystalline silica, ethylene glycol, toluene, or any other product suspected to cause cancer.

Farrow and Ball (*www.farrow-ball.com*) uses naturally

occurring pigments and ingredients like linseed oil and china clay and has recently significantly reduced the solvent in its products. Most of the paint in their line is low or no VOC.

Milk Paint (*www.milkpaint.com*) produces organic, biodegradable paint made with food ingredients. The paint is totally free of VOCs, lead, radioactive materials, petroleum by products, synthetic preservatives, and other harmful poisons. Their paint is not combustible if a fire occurs.

Yolo Colorhouse (*www.yolocolorhouse.com*) produces no VOC paints, uses 100 percent post-consumer recycled paper, printed with soy ink for their labels, and the lightest possible 100 percent post-consumer recycled content packaging. Wash water from their plants is recycled back into their paint and they use wind power at their headquarters. They provide poster-sized swatches so there are less "Wow, the chip didn't look like that" moments.

Mythic Paint (*www.mythicpaint.com*) is nontoxic, durable, and safe for pets, people, and the earth. The site has a paint estimator to help you calculate the correct amount of paint needed and avoid waste. The company is certified by Green Wise.

AFM Safecoat (*www.afmsafecoat.com*) has been working for over twenty-five years to produce a zero VOC product that does not contain heavy metals, formaldehyde, solvents, and other harmful chemicals. They participate in the Degree of Green program in which retailers are able to provide data sheets of products' green qualities, similar to nutritional labels on food products.

Sherwin-Williams' Harmony brand (*www.sherwin-williams.com*) is a Greenguard certified, no VOC paint with antimicrobial properties. The Harmony brand is a reasonably priced, durable acrylic paint.

Natura, from Benjamin Moore (*www.benjamin-moore.com*) is a no VOC paint that is virtually odorless and exceeds industry standards for environmental safety. It's quick drying, allowing you to use the room the same day you paint, and can qualify for LEED points. The Aura paint line is an affordable no VOC paint option with over 3,330 color choices. Any sheen is washable and the reps will provide you with a serious sample kit.

Tile

Recycled tiles come in glass, ceramic, and porcelain made from recycled glass and pre-consumer industrial waste. Unfortunately the variety of size, color, and texture found in conventional tiles has not crossed over into the recycled product. The good news is that more and more vendors are adding recycled content tiles to their lines. As with all green products, make sure the adhesives and backing are nontoxic.

All tiles in Hakatai's Ashland-e series (*www.hakatai.com*) is comprised of 30 to 70 percent glass from recycled bottles and other glass waste. The waste glass is a mix of 90 percent post-consumer material and 10 percent pre-consumer waste. They offer a skid resistant finish on their mosaics for wet areas.

Oceanside Glasstile (*www.glasstile.com*) features glass mosaic tiles made of between 30 and 94 percent recycled glass. The site has a chart stating the exact amount of recycled material in each color.

Mosaic tiles from Trend's Feel line (*www.trendin-green.com*) are made from 78 percent post-consumer recycled glass (bottles and glass containers) and are available in thirty-five colors.

Palm Springs can get pretty hot with summer temperatures upward of 115 degrees. An icy white mosaic tile was installed in this powder room to create a cooling effect. The cabinet is made from FSC-certified wood and eco-friendly stain. The mosaics, from Hakatai, are from their recycled glass line. Fluorescent wall sconces offer a soothing glow against the tiled wall.

Powder Room by Lori Dennis, photo by Mark Tanner

It's undeniable that any well-installed plaster wall is irresistible to the touch, but Earth Plaster walls are actually good for your skin. The clay they use actually releases and absorbs moisture as it is needed in the interior. They're also made from natural pigments that have breathtaking hues. If your budget allows, this is one of the most scrumptious interior splurges you can buy. Plus, added moisture in the room where you sleep helps to hydrate skin (less wrinkles).

Bedrock Industries (*www.bedrockindustries.com*) sells handmade tiles made from 100 percent recycled glass and raw source materials. No chemical pigments are used for color. What I really like about this source is that they offer a wide variety of sizes (hexagon, subway, and thin breadsticks) and colors and the products look amazing. Packaging for shipping is made of 100 percent recyclable material and they support local elementary school bottle drives. Earnings go to sponsor educational field trips for the students.

Based in San Jose, California, Fire Clay Tile (*www.fireclaytile.com*) provides beautiful, durable, recycled content tile manufactured with sustainable methods.

The glass they use for their tile is from contaminated consumer glass (think glass jars with peanut butter still in them). This glass, used in their Debris Series, would otherwise be unrecyclable. Because you don't see this size in a recycled product often, I have to point out the Claymonde line, which features super-sized wall tile as big as 35"x70" in thirty-two colors. Although tiles are made to order, they sometimes wind up with seconds or overstock. These materials are sold to nonprofits at a 90 percent discount.

Porcelanosa (*www.porcelanosa-usa.com*) uses nontoxic glaze on all tiles and 100 percent recycled material to ship them. The plastic wrap it uses is recycled back into plastic wrap. There is a pallet return policy to minimize the consumption of pallets. This vendor offers tiles that resemble wood planks, a perfect solution for blending your indoor and outdoor spaces.

Eco Spec Tile (*www.ecospectile.com*) has nine different lines of ceramic and porcelain tiles which contain up to 45 percent pre- and post-consumer materials. The Green Tech and Mikado lines even have a solid white colored tile, which is extremely difficult to find when you're looking for a tile with recycled content. The company recycles and reuses all water in the production process and ships with recycled material packaging.

Plaster

Earth-based plasters are the healthiest wall finish. Natural clay plaster allows a wall to absorb and release moisture as needed. This amazing self-adjustment in the humidity levels of a room helps to ensure that the space is comfortable for its occupants and unlikely to develop mold.

American Clay (*www.americanclay.com*) is really the only company I use. They have been in the business of healthy walls for the past twenty-five years and have perfected it. Their line offers multiple finishes and a wide variety of colors. Any plaster professional can apply it, it's easy to repair when damaged, and the product looks simply elegant.

Wallcover

For many years manufacturers offered PVC-based vinyl "wallpaper," which was cheap, extremely durable, and easy to clean. Eventually it became known that vinyl wallcovering offgases plasticizers (known endocrine disruptors) into your living space and into landfills when discarded. It is ironic that this is what lined nursing homes and hospital rooms for years. In the past decade light has been shed on the detrimental effects that PVC-based wallcover has on indoor air quality. As a response, an entire green wallcover industry seemed to sprout overnight. Along with paint, environmentally friendly wallcover is

This pattern from Innovations is one of the prettiest wallcovers in existence. It's sparkly, swirly, sultry, and sustainable. This may be the most striking example of how luxury, respect for resources and healthy interiors can co-exist.

one of the most plentiful, easy-to-find surface materials. These new products do not contain heavy metals or PVC. They are made from rapidly renewable sources like cork, grasses, and other plant fibers.

Even though most natural fibers are breathable, it is still best to avoid wallcover in humid areas, like bathrooms and home spas. If moisture condenses behind the wallcover, it can result in mold and rot.

Finally, when the wallcover is applied, you must be certain that the green paper you specify is pasted with an equally environmentally friendly paste or glue. It completely defeats the purpose of a purchasing a health-based wallcover when the adhesive behind it is offgassing toxins into the room. The VOCs from the glue can literally get you high and not in a good way.

Innovations (*www.innovations.com*) was the first company to develop a line of environmentally friendly wallcover, which is as tough as it is beautiful. The Innvironments line is made from renewable or recycled materials, is PVC free, and nontoxic. The company has reduced 30 percent of waste at their plants.

Judit Gueth (*www.juditgueth.com*) specializes in bold graphics and interesting color combinations. Her product is made from strong, non-woven substrates making removing paper so much easier. It actually comes off in one piece so it doesn't damage the wall and the paper can be reused. Judit's wallcover is prepasted in a clay-based adhesive, so dipping it in the water for ten seconds actually activates the paste.

MDC Wallcoverings (*www.mdcwall.com*) has everything you would expect from an Angela Adams design, minus the toxins and PVC. The Angela Adams line is breathable, made from 100 percent post-consumer waste, is Greenguard certified, and printed with water-based inks without heavy metals. Products are packaged in recycled paper.

Mod Green Pod (*www.modgreenpod.com*) features vinyl-free wallpapers that use water-based inks on a cellulose paper and give the paper a water-based glaze that can tolerate light wiping. Lovely designs that work all over a playful home.

Carnegie Fabrics' Xorel and Surface iQ lines (*www.carnegiefabrics.com*) have sublime collections

Modular Arts wall panels transform ordinary walls into extraordinary experiences. This home, owned by a DJ and a club promoter, sees its fair share of guests who expect to be wowed. When you look at this dining room, I'm sure you'll agree it's something else! The panels are free of toxic chemicals, easy to install, and can be painted, but also look fabulous in their natural state, as shown in this photo.

Dining room by Lori Dennis, photo by Ken Hayden

which have achieved the Cradle to Cradle rating.

Concertex's Eco Skin SF and Olenox lines (*www.concertex.com*) offer sophisticated transitional patterns on PVC free wallcovering.

Inhabit (*www.inhabiliving.com*) features Chrysalis Wall flats, made from renewable bamboo pulp, which don't offgas. They can be painted and are easy to mount with adhesive on the back.

Faux Stone

Unless you can specify a natural stone that is abundant and mined within 500 miles of your project, a greener choice is faux stone. Using a faux stone product on the walls can save an enormous amount of labor, cost, energy, and natural resources. The advances in technology have resulted in a product that closely resembles nature. In fact, I won the *Southern Accents*/ASID best green design award this year with a bedroom featuring a wall covered in faux stone. If it passed the approval of Southern style guru, *Southern Accents* Editor in Chief Karen Carroll, you can feel confident about using it.

Eldorado Stone (*www.eldoradostone.com*) has five manufacturing plants strategically located throughout the country, which means that 78 percent of the United States population lives within 500 miles of an Eldorado plant. They recycle water in the manufacturing process and are committed to sourcing local, raw materials made with pre- and post-consumer waste products. The product contributes thermal mass to walls, helping to insulate for heating and cooling and is half the weight of stone, resulting in reduced shipping pollution. The product is long lasting, with a fifty-year warranty. It also helps you to qualify for LEED points.

Renaissance (*www.ecospectile.com*) is man-made sandstone, which includes up to 25 percent post-industrial recycled materials like silica and mineral oxide pigments. During processing water is recycled and reused, and manufacturing is nontoxic. The company implements a facility-wide recycling program and packages products in recycled materials.

Wall Panels

Installing wall panels provides a dramatic way to dress a wall or separate areas in a room. When panels are installed directly on walls, they add to the thermal mass, which helps regulate heat and cold air exchange. Wall panel products can be made from eco-friendly materials and are an attractive and welcome change to paint and wallcover.

Modular Arts (*www.modulararts.com*) has a cast rock, noncombustible, no glue, no plastics, no VOC, no formaldehyde wall panel that mounts directly on to existing drywall or substrate. In new construction the product takes the place of drywall and insulates at the same time. It comes in various patterns and can be painted any color. The product is highly durable, safe, and healthy.

Kirei Coco Tiles (*www.kireiusa.com*) are one of my new favorite wall finishes. For years we've been seeing the stacked stone look and Kirei has this fresh new way to adorn the walls with woven coconut panels. They're made from reclaimed coconut shells, low VOC resins, and sustainably harvested wood backer. They can be used for walls, millwork, and cabinetry to help you get LEED points.

Armourcoat (*www.usa.armourcoat.com*) is a global powerhouse in decorative finishes, from luxurious Venetian plaster to textured wall finishes and stone-like cast products. Most products have low or zero VOC content and incorporate pre- and post-consumer recycled material, qualifying for inclusion within LEED projects.

3Form Panels (*www.3-form.com*) are a striking solution to separating space in kitchens, bedrooms, and bathrooms. The product is nontoxic and contains 40 percent post industrial recycled content, is available in a wide range of colors, and is translucent enough to let light shine through. I've also used them very successfully in the place of glass panels in doors and cabinets. Now the company offers frames for these panels, which, trust me, makes your projects much easier. Their Varia Ecoresin line is eligible for LEED points.

COUNTERS AND BACKSPLASHES

For our purposes three things should be considered when installing counters and backsplashes. Is the material environmentally friendly, is it durable, and is it easy to clean? A green installation will consist of a product that meets all of these criteria. Many times a homeowner is seduced by the words "natural stone" and incorrectly thinks those words represent a better product. When I explain the toll "natural stone" has on the environment and the required upkeep, they become more willing to look at my green choice. The composite stone materials available today closely resemble stone, but do not require the maintenance of stone or the extraction and transportation consequences usually associated with natural stone. To convert the non-believers, I recently did a sample test of a grey limestone and engineered quartz. My subjects were shocked that they could not tell the difference.

Enviroglas (*www.enviroglasproducts.com*) is an American company at the forefront of design and recycling. Granite comes from far away. It's heavy and requires a lot of energy to mine it, shape it, and get it from places like Turkey to your project. Synthetic, recycled countertops utilize broken glass and porcelain, suspended in a resin, to create gorgeous, durable surfaces perfect for cooking, eating, and living. They are installed and work just like granite, but greener.

Caesar Stone (*www.caesarstoneus.com*) was the first solid surface company to make an environmental commitment back in 1987. The Greenguard-certified product uses recycled content and recycles industrial raw material and 97 percent of water used in processing. They avoid using hazardous substances and the counter tops are impervious to mold and microbes.

The ECO brand (*www.ecobyconsentino.com*) is both Cradle to Cradle and Greenguard certified, is a durable

This is one of the most eco-friendly kitchens I've ever designed. The counters are Caesarstone, with cabinets by Valcucine. Gaggenau's greenest of appliances were installed and reclaimed oak panels adorn the walls. In addition to a serene palette that lets the food shine, my favorite part of the space is the floor to ceiling windows that allow natural light to dance throughout the kitchen. Being in this space is an utter joy. Green design should make you feel good and this room does exactly that.

surface made of 75 percent recycled content composed of post-industrial or post-consumer materials, and is bound by an environmentally friendly resin which comes in part from corn oil. ECO is an ideal substitute for natural or engineered stone.

EnviroPLANK and EnviroSLAB terrazzo tiles and slabs (*www.enviroglasproducts.com*) are made of post-consumer and post-industrial recycled glass. The product is made from 75 percent recycled glass from local recy-

cling programs for minimal transportation impact. The product is resistant to chips, stains, burns, and chemicals and has zero VOCs and virtually no emissions. Maintenance of the product requires only water, mild cleaner, and no wax. It is designed to last a lifetime, but can be ground up for a new floor if desired.

In addition to recycled content slabs and environmentally conscious practices in their manufacturing plants, Consentino, Silestone's parent company (*www.silestoneusa.com*), cooperates with the quarries they mine to restore the environment to its original landscape.

The Ice Stone brand (*www.ecospectile.com*) is Cradle to Cradle certified and made from 100 percent recycled glass. The glass counter top is mixed with cement for a concrete surface. It's free from VOCs, plastics, resins, and you can earn up to 6 LEED points by using it.

Coverings Etc.'s Bio-Glass counter tops (*www.coveringsetc.com*) are made from 100 percent recycled and

Bedroom by Lori Dennis, photo by Christian Romero

2008 Southern Accents green category winner featuring El Dorado Stone, Anna Sova linens, custom bed made of FSC-certified wood, and AFM Safecoat stain, vintage lamps, and painting by Tony Caputo. Clearly the bedroom would not be the same without the dramatic use of stone. The twist is that this stone is generally applied to an exterior. With no reason to limit ourselves, the client and I decided to bring the outdoors in. Two magazine covers and the Southern Accents award confirmed that we made the right choice.

recyclable glass bottles and stemware. The product has Cradle to Cradle Silver Tier certification.

Ace Concrete (*www.aceconcrete*.com) uses an aggregate in their counter tops, sinks, and fireplaces that comes from renewable Monterey beach sand. The sand is polished by the ocean and becomes non-angular which eliminates containments that weaken conventional cements. The result is a very dense, strong-finished product that lasts for a very long time.

Trend (*www.trendingreen.com*) manufactures two recycled-content slab products: Prezioso, made from their own production waste of glass mosaic, and Cristallino, made from Pyrex glass from windshields, rearview mirrors, and lights.

SINKS AND TUBS

Using reclaimed or recycled sinks and tubs can accomplish green and aesthetic design goals. It keeps old products out of landfills, eliminates the need for raw materials or production of new products, and can make a charming interior style. Water conservation can be accomplished by installing screw-in aerators to control water flow (older toilets that flush with more than 1.6 gallons of water should not be installed). To prevent lead poisoning make sure that any painted product made before 1970 is tested for lead.

There is a lot of scrap iron in the world. Most of it is just sitting in landfills, slowly oxidizing and rusting away. Kohler (*www.us.kohler.com*) has a full of line of tubs, sinks, fixtures, and accessories crafted from 97 percent recycled iron. They melt down products headed for the waste stream and make them into bubble tubs and sinks. It's possible the tub you sink into tonight was once a bumper for a '67 Ford Fairlane.

CABINETS

Many affordable conventional cabinets are made with pressed particleboard and veneers. Quite often the particleboard contains formaldehyde binders which can offgas for the life of the cabinets. To make matters worse, the clear finishes commonly applied to cabinets are made from urea-formaldehyde resins. This is probably not the healthiest place to store food, dishes, and utensils. The exceptions to this rule are European cabinets, made of high-density fiberboard. Mandated by law in Europe, the chipboard that is used has to comply with a set standard of formaldehyde emissions. The European standard for chipboard is titled E1, confirming emission levels that are acceptable. In addition to the chipboard, European manufacturers use finishes and glue that comply with emission standards. Wheatboard covered in eco-friendly veneers is also a good solution to achieving affordably priced, environmentally sound cabinets.

When you have a bigger budget for solid wood cabinets, make sure the wood is FSC certified. The paints and finishing materials must also be no VOC and nontoxic.

Reusing existing cabinets is the greenest option of all. New doors and hardware can be added to existing boxes to achieve an entirely new look. If the cabinet configuration and door style still works but needs updating, consider painting or refinishing. If you are removing cabinets, donate or relocate to a storage area to avoid having them end up a landfill.

Finally, remember that a smooth cabinet surface is easier and quicker to clean.

Valcucine (*www.valcucinena.com*), the greenest of all European cabinets, went so far as to found a reforestation group, BioForest. Their cabinetry uses up to 80 percent less material than competing products. They are free of formaldehyde and use only nontoxic, citrus oil finishes. Recently they introduced Invitrum. Its glass doors, cabinets, and countertops make up the world's first eco-friendly, zero-emission, 100 percent recyclable kitchen cabinets. The bases of the units are made with recycled aluminum and glass, which are assembled with mechanical joinery so no glue is needed. The glass panels are only 10 mm thick which replaces the need for double panels, resulting in fewer materials. The cabinets are made to last a life-time, and at the end of their lifecycle, they are labeled for 100 percent recycling.

Italian Kitchen Design (*www.ikdusa.com*) features attractive and affordable Italian cabinets made with European environmental standards, imported top of the line veneers, and pressure laminates.

The core materials of Humabuilt cabinets (*www.humabuilt.com*) are renewable and recyclable, manufactured without formaldehyde. They are also very careful about the adhesives they use and they have passed some of the most stringent air quality standards in the United States.

Sleek, strong, and sustainable describe the flexible kitchen systems from Bazzèo (*www.bazzeo.com*). Customizable cabinets, drawers, and storage pieces are crafted from rapidly renewable and recycled materials, including wheatboard, aluminum, stainless steel, and cer-tified woods finished with wood veneers, aluminum, or laminate panels, and low- to no-emission lacquers. Bazzèo says it transforms all manufacturing waste into new products and plants a tree for each new order.

Kirei (*www.kireiusa.com*) is a leader in green wheat-board. The Kirei product often exceeds the characteristics of commercially available MDF but it comes from a renewable source and uses nontoxic adhesives. When you use the Kirei wheatboard instead of conventional MDF you can earn LEED points for rapidly renewable material, recycled content, and indoor quality.

Lyptus (*www.lyptus.com*) sells a new species of wood developed for cabinetry. It grows in about half the time as other cabinet wood but has the same beneficial qualities, no formaldehyde binders, and is visually attractive. Not a lot of cabinetmakers will have heard of this material, but they should have no problem working with it. For successful examples, go to *www.showplacewood.com*.

Cabinetmaker Tonusa (*www.tonusa.com*) has an new green cabinet line and recognizes the need to care for our environment for the benefit of future generations. Tonusa uses environmentally responsible raw materials in its products such as wood boards that meet stringent European standards, imported premium laminates and veneers.

Treefrog Veneer (*www.treefrogveneer.com*) carries a complete selection of forty-nine real wood veneer laminates, representing the most beautiful wood species in the world. A One Percent for the Planet member, they practice sustainable forestry, use water-based dyes and stains, which are free of chrome, and follow E1 European limits for formaldehyde emission. The production facility is located in Massachusetts.

Brookside Veneers (*www.veneers.com*) has had a strong commitment to the environment for over thirty years, from the harvest and manufacturing processes to the recyclable paper products they purchase. The company has made substantial investments in state-of–the-art machinery to reduce dust and fumes to preserve air quality. Wastewater from dyeing vats is processed back into clean water and wood scraps are put back into production. Their veneers have achieved FSC certification and the company donates portions of their profits to organizations promoting forest renewal and health.

HARDWARE

World famous Liz's Antique Hardware (*www.lahardware.com*) provides window, door, and furniture hardware and accessories from circa 1860 to 1970. Everything is neatly organized, making the process of using reclaimed hardware as easy as picking something new.

Sun Valley Bronze (*www.sunvalleybronze.com*), manufactured in Sun Valley, Idaho, practices environ-mental responsibility by using green sand technology in the casting process. It participates in metal scrap and office recycling programs and provides healthy working conditions for its employees. It uses 90—95 percent recy-cled content materials in its white bronze and silicon bronze products. Bronze also has natural antimicrobial and self-decontaminating properties.

Rocky Mountain Hardware (*www.rockymountainhardware.com*), a family-owned and operated business located in Sun Valley, Idaho, uses 90 percent pre-consumer and 50 percent post-consumer recycled material to create all of their products. The company headquarters are housed in a LEED certified building. They practice conservation in their daily business activities including: recycled water, waste recycling, and naturally lit working spaces.

green Sage (*www.greensage*.com) offers styles ranging from bamboo designs to 100 percent recycled glass knobs and lead-free pewter knobs, pulls, and bathroom accessories.

Anna Sova (*www.annasova.com*) sells drapery hard-ware made in the United States from 100 percent post-consumer recycled aluminum and recycled glass, and is finished with no VOC products. Hardware is shipped in minimal packaging.

SEALERS, FINISHES, AND ADHESIVES

After spending the time and money to select green finishes, one of the big mistakes many people make is attaching or finishing them with toxic products. Natural products are a better alternative to conventional petroleum-based fin-ishes. These healthier options have not yet been perfected and you may sometimes have to sacrifice moisture resistance and an easy installation process for healthier air quality. It's a trade most of us are willing to make.

One of my favorite surface materials is veneer. It adds richness and dimension to interiors reminiscent of the work of '30s French masters like Ruhlmann and Jean-Michel Frank. Brookside and Tree Frog carry exquisite and downright funky variations of the best that nature has to offer. The companies exhibit environmentally responsible practices and harvest sustainable materials. The Tree Frog veneered bar featured in this photo is an example of the magnificence you can achieve when you apply veneer to a surface. Caesarstone counters and a cellar of almost 200 bottles of sommelier-selected wines leave you wanting even more.

ONE-STOP SHOPS

The following four shops are comprehensive resources for one-stop shopping. Many of the products listed in this book can be found at one of these green vendors.

Ellen Strickland, founder of Livingreen (*www.livingreen.com*), is a pioneer in the green building environment, supporting a healthier existence for people, animals, and the planet. Her stores and Web site are places where people can learn about sustainable products and living. She writes, speaks on panels throughout the country, and hosts educational events at all three of her retail locations. Ellen and Livingreen sponsored me on my first eco-friendly showcase home, filling the entire three bedroom home with accessories, art, and linens. This showcase event helped solidify my status as a green designer, and I can never thank her enough for the green spirit of generosity she practices everyday.

The mission of 'g' Green Design (*www.ggreendesign.com*) is to provide excellent quality, affordable, and responsible green building materials. The Web site is easy to navigate and has an abundance of eco-friendly information and products. They sponsor workshops and lectures ranging from green building to green retailing.

Epoxy Green (*www.epoxygreen.com*) offers sustainable building and design products for residential and commercial applications. They regularly host events to showcase cutting edge products and help the community come together to learn about green living.

Green Depot (*www.greendepot.com*) has showrooms in Brooklyn, Newark, Philadelphia, Boston, Greenport, Chicago, Albany, and Manhattan and is adding locations as I write. In addition to a comprehensive selection of paints, finishes, carpeting, flooring, cabinets, and countertops this retailer offers a wide selection of green home products, building materials, books, lighting, and a baby shop. They are committed to affordable, green living solutions accessible for all types of budgets.

Livos (*www.livos.co.uk*) offers low VOC wood stains and finishes and technical data sheets on all of their products, which give relevant information of application ranges and product contents.

AFM Safecoat (*www.afmsafecoat.com*) has eliminated toxic ingredients such as solvents, heavy metals, chemical residues, and formaldehyde from their products. Paint, stain, and finish products literally contain a "safe coat" with a molecular formulation designed to seal surfaces greatly reducing any offgassing.

5 INTERIOR PLANTS

Most people know that plants can make a space look better but are unaware that they can also improve the air quality in a room and a person's health. According to the Environmental Protection Agency most Americans spend 90 percent of their lives indoors and interiors are five to ten times more polluted than the exterior.

INTERIOR PLANTS AND INDOOR AIR QUALITY

When I first heard that our interior spaces were more polluted than outside, I didn't believe it. Not my house, I'm a clean freak. I don't even wear shoes inside. But even my extremely clean house is filled with toxins from the plastic (which seems to be everywhere I look), computers, my television, printer inks, dry cleaned clothes, and construction materials.

I live in a moderate climate so I don't use air conditioning and I rarely turn on the heat. Most of the year I have the windows open for a portion of each day to allow fresh air and sunlight to flood my home. I've done this since I was a kid and my brother named me the "fresh air freak." My furnishings, window treatments, and rugs have been specified with green materials in mind. I only use nontoxic cleaning products. Even still, there are toxins in my haven that can cause headaches, nausea, sore throat, dry skin, itchy eyes, and even a loss of concentration. There is actually a term for the way a polluted interior can make you feel. It's called Sick Building Syndrome. One way to combat these symptoms is with indoor plants. They are known to clean the air, replenish it with oxygen helping to reduce negative physical symptoms, and even make people more calm. Plants are literally the greenest way of improving indoor air quality.

What specifically do plants do to improve indoor air quality? Rooms with plants have been measured as showing up to 60 percent less airborne molds and bacteria than rooms with no plants. They suck the toxins out of the environment and act as purifying organs, like the kidneys or lungs of the house. Amazingly, the plants absorb the contaminants into their leaves and transfer them to their roots where they digest them as food. They do this by releasing phytochemicals, which act as moisture, into the air in order to "catch" the dirty air around them, which they pull down into the roots. By releasing and aborsbing humidity in the environment, plants are able to aid in regulating a comfortable climate.

Humans have also been known to become sick when humidity levels drop, so plants are essentially helping us to ward off colds. English ivy is said to be one of the best plants to fight off colds. Small openings on the underside of a plant's leaves release moisture into the air, boosting humidity level helping to alleviate cold symptoms. Because of English ivy's high volume of leaves, horticulturists recommend it as one of the most effective cold-fighting plants. On the flip side, too much moisture can be a bad thing if mold occurs. Mold becomes a problem when humidity levels become too high. Mold can wreak havoc on a structure and our bodies. Again, by helping to regulate humidity, plants help to control mold.

Research has shown that plants can improve our mood by increasing positive feelings. This improves creativity by producing higher dopamine levels which control the flow of information to our brains. By also reducing noise pollution (neighbors, gardeners, car alarms) they allow us to concentrate and use our creativity. Because evolution has taught humans that plants are essential for survival, just seeing a plant can reduce stress levels by inducing a calming effect. It has also been shown that in hot months, plants have a cooling effect. They are even said to produce a healthy drop in heart rate. Studies have shown people in rooms with plants had a four-point drop in their systolic heart rate after taking a stress test versus people taking the same test with no plants in the room. They had only a two-point drop.

Let's face it, I am in the business of making rooms look good and interiors with plants have been perceived as more expensive looking than those without. So in addition to purifying the air we breathe these living organisms help us to live better.

Which plants are the best for clean interior air, and how many do you need? All plants will help to clean the environment but some will work harder than others at digesting the microbes that live in their potting soil and reversing the effects of the VOCs in your indoor environment. VOCs emitted from paint, furniture, carpets, and other carcinogenic offgassers in your environment include: formaldehyde, toluene, xylene, tricholorethylene, ammonia, carbon monoxide, and benzene. These are just a few of the toxins you live with and breathe in everyday. Formaldehyde is released by draperies, upholstery, paper towels, facial tissue, nail polish remover, grocery bags, plywood, particleboard, paints, stains, caulking, and varnishes. Xylene and toluene are released by human breath, computer screens, photocopiers, printers, stains, and varnishes. Benzene is released by tobacco smoke, printers, copiers, floor and wall coverings, particleboard, caulking, adhesives, paints, stains, and varnishes. Ammonia is released by

[1] Orchids minimize xylene and toluene.

[2] English ivy aids in the reduction of benzene levels and formaldehyde.

[3] Bamboo combats formaldehyde levels.

[4] Ficus is able to remove high concentrations of formaldehyde, benzene and triclorethylene. Ficus is resistant to many household insects and will grow in full or semi-sun.

[5] Ferns remove formaldehyde and ammonia. They are easy to care for because they require little water, but they must be misted a few times a week or the leaves will brown and drop. They thrive in indirect light. Ferns may be one of the oldest groups of plants dating back to prehistoric times.

[6] Palms (specifically Areca and Lady Palm) reduce ammonia, formaldehyde, xylene, and toluene. The Areca is consistently rated among the best household plants for removing toxins and should be kept in semi-shade. The Lady Palm is highly resistant to most plant insects, slow to grow, easy to maintain and should also be kept in semi-shade.

[7] Peace Lilies can add up to 5 percent humidity to a room and reduce benzene, trichloroethylene, and acetone levels. Their best work is done in mid-light to shade.

[8] Philodendrons can thrive without a lot of natural light, so they are ideal for darker areas of the interior where other plants cannot survive. Philodendrons are particularly effective in removing formaldehyde.

[9] My personal favorites are succulents. They are extremely low maintenance and require little water. There are many varieties that bloom in brilliant colors. Since these plants are usually thought of as an exterior group, it is a delightful surprise to see them thriving indoors. Jade plants, known as the "money tree" are particularly wonderful for interiors. They can be potted as small table plants or allowed to grow into large trees. At certain times of the year, they bloom with clusters of small pink flowers, a truly perfect sight.

cleaning agents, human breath, printers, and photocopiers.

NASA contracted an environmental engineer to perform a study on houseplants combating pollution. He exposed various plants to high levels of chemicals and found that the houseplants were able to remove 87 percent of air toxins in a twenty-four-hour period. Based on this study, NASA recommends fifteen to eighteen plants (in six- to eight-inch diameter pots) in an 1,800 square foot home to purify indoor air.

The following is a list of some of the best plants for indoor air quality and human health and well-being.

Gerber Daisies are known to reduce formaldehyde and benzene.

Dracaena (corn plant) removes formaldehyde.

Spider Plants remove benzene and formadelhyde.

Janet Craig is a tropical shrub that grows eight to twelve feet tall. It has green leaves which are sometimes cultivated to a grey-green color. The plant has been shown by NASA to help remove formaldehyde, xylene, and toluene. One NASA study showed three Janet Craigs in a 130-square-foot room were able to cut 70 percent of the VOCs. This plant can tolerate dimly lit areas, but does best in semi-shade.

If you kill everything, snake plants are easy to maintain. Even in windowless rooms, they are effective at reducing indoor toxins.

The EPA and NASA are in agreement about the fact that indoor air quality is worse than outdoor. However the EPA says that it would take hundreds of plants to duplicate the toxin removing effects produced in the NASA studies. No matter who is right, it is a fact that plants add oxygen and humidity to the air, which has proven health benefits. All you have to do is look at plants and flowers and you find yourself relaxing, sometimes even experiencing the corners of your mouth turning up—that has to be good for you.

CUT FLOWERS

Who doesn't love to get flowers? They're gorgeous, they smell good and make an interior look magazine ready. Cut flowers are an easy hostess gift and generally make anyone happy. But there are some dirty secrets that no one ever tells you about cut flowers. About 80 percent of cut flowers are grown in South America, Africa, and Southeast Asia. Most of the time they are grown in greenhouses that use pesticides, herbicides, and fungicides, which are banned in the United States. These include DDT and methyl-bromide. The people who work in these greenhouses come into contact with these chemicals on a daily basis. Some of the symptoms they experience are skin and respiratory illness, birth defects, and impaired vision. If that isn't bad enough, the chemicals they are using are flushed into the earth and ground water, causing serious problems for animal, bird, and fish populations. The pollution released into the ground water also reduces levels of potable water.

These flowers are then sent thousands of miles, mostly to the United States, using millions of gallons of fuel and releasing large amounts of pollution into the environment on their journey. Once they reach the United States they are sprayed with even more chemicals to kill any foreign insects. Even flowers grown in the United States, which don't have to travel as far and don't use banned chemicals,

Succulent

Various succulents

PLANTS still use plenty of toxic pesticides and fertilizers that hurt our environment, people, and animals. Check out this entertaining cartoon video that perfectly illustrates my point: *www.lifegoggles.com/3597/the-environmental-cost-of-cut-flowers/*

(This could be occurring with plants as well, but plants are the lesser of two evils as you can buy one plant that will last for many decades.)

For those of you who cannot bear to give up cut flowers, and I'm one of you, there is an alternative. Buy local organic flowers. Most of the time you can find seasonal varieties at your local farmers market and they are usually pretty affordable.

If you have the space, try planting a cut flower garden. Hydrangea is one of the most beautiful flowers and the plant really grows like a weed (for most of the late spring until fall outside) in partial shade. In the living rooms chapter I discuss outdoor gardens, so more on that subject soon.

One last option is artificial flowers and plants. I generally don't go this route as I am a plant lover with two green thumbs. However, if plants are hard for you or your clients, there are some incredibly realistic arrangements you can buy. Some of the best ones I've seen are from the Diane James collection. I'm really not a big fan of "fake" flowers, but hers are really stunning.

PLANTS

Gardens Alive (*www.gardensalive.com*) is an environmentally responsible retailer of flower bulbs and seeds.

ARTIFICIAL PLANTS AND FLOWERS

Diane James (*www.dianejames.com*) is a couture source for artificial floral arrangements, orchids, and topiaries.

Aldik Home (*www.aldikhome.com*) has a large collection of silk flowers, trees, and containers.

Plant Pusher (*www.plantpusher.com*) features modern, lifelike floral arrangements, beaded botanicals, and interior landscaping.

ORGANIC CUT FLOWERS

California Organic Flowers (*www.californiaorganicflowers.com*) sells certified organic cut flowers with next-day delivery.

Local Harvest (*www.localharvest.org*) is a family farm cooperative that supplies flowers, produce, meats, and other products directly to local communities

Diamond Organics (*www.diamondorganics.com*) sells -flowers grown in California and Hawaii exclusively by organic farms.

6 APPLIANCES AND PLUMBING FIXTURES

When selecting appliances and plumbing fixtures for a green home pay close attention to water and energy conservation features in addition to performance. Energy Star's rating system has taken a lot of the guesswork out of selecting appliances that don't waste energy. The Water Sense label will lead you in the right direction for water efficient fixtures. When you're buying new items, make sure to select quality materials that will last for decades. If you're purchasing salvaged materials be certain that you are not sacrificing water or energy efficiency.

Designing in a water-wise manner will be required by law in the coming years. Studies say that in the next decade water shortages will be a serious worldwide problem. Our current water resources will not be sufficient anymore. If we want the next generation to have fresh water we will need to take a new approach toward usage and waste.

Kitchen by Lori Dennis, photo by Roi Yerushalmi

This kitchen proves the point that you don't have to spend a small fortune to have a gorgeous, green kitchen. Reasonably priced Energy Star rated dishwasher, cooktop and hood fill the space lavishly and live up to the expectations of the homeowners.

CONSERVATION IS KEY

Every time I brush my teeth and wash my face, I turn off the faucet between lathering and rinsing and do not let the water run. I can't imagine watching clean water just run down a drain. Most people who have grown up in desert climates like California have had to conserve water at one time or another and it's become routine for us. The utilities in California have just mandated a 20 percent increase in water prices. You can bet any Californian who didn't watch their usage before will soon start. Homeowners will be in a big rush to fix leaky faucets when it hits them in the wallet.

But what about places that seem to have an endless supply of fresh water? Do they conserve? Should they conserve? I had a layover in Zurich, Switzerland, and used the bathroom in the business class lounge to wash up after the transatlantic flight from Los Angeles. An American woman was using the sink next to me. She turned the water up full blast and let it run as she washed her face and brushed her teeth. She left it running at full blast and left to use the toilet. I stood there for a second in shock, feeling very uncomfortable. I reached over and turned off "her" faucet. When she returned from the toilet, she asked me if I turned off her water. I said yes, so she asked me why. I told her I couldn't stand to see the

fresh water being wasted. She laughed at me and said, "It's Switzerland, they have plenty of water."

What people don't seem to realize is that there are too many people on this planet to waste fresh water. The water that comes from the tap is not limitless. Water is a finite resource, which is getting expensive. As we continue to pollute it with manufacturing, waste, and toxic chemicals, clean water becomes scarce. The human population is growing faster than our fresh water supply and will not continue to meet our needs in the next century if we do not change our ways. I often wonder why, with a planet that is made up of three quarters of water, albeit saltwater, we haven't come up with a better solution for desalinization. But that's a discussion for another day and still not an excuse to waste water.

Wasting energy by using non-renewable resources negatively effects the environment by depleting valuable resources that cannot be replaced, creating air pollution and emitting greenhouse gases. Most of the energy used to power American households comes from sources such as coal- and oil-fed power plants. The carbon emissions from these plants wreak havoc in our atmosphere and are said to cause human illness and speed up global warming. Specifying appliances that use energy in the most efficient manner helps to slow down carbon emissions.

The following Web sites compare water and energy usage. Energy Star (*www.energystar.gov/index.cfm?c=appliances.pr_appliances*) lists all of the Energy Star products

For those of you with high-dollar budgets, take a look at Gaggenau's suite of top of the line green appliances. They show like art in the kitchen and work like a dream. If you enjoy that "hidden" look, they accept cabinet panels exceptionally well.

Kitchen by Lori Dennis, photo by Ken Hayden

available on the market. The site gives information on how much energy and water are saved per manufacturer or model number.

The American Council for an Energy Efficient Economy (*www.aceee.org*) gives energy ratings of appliances.

Green-e (*www.green-e.org*) provides customers clear information about green electricity products to help them make informed purchases and encourage the use of products that minimize air pollution and reduce greenhouse gas emissions.

Consumer Reports' Greener Choices (*www.greenerchoices.org*) informs consumers about environmentally friendly products and offers reliable, practical sources of information on how to buy green and avoid "greenwashed" products.

TOILETS

Toilet flushing is the single largest use of water in most homes. In 1992 Federal law mandated that new residential toilets use no more than 1.6 gallons per flush. Understandably consumers were concerned about the ability of these "new" toilets to get the job done properly. The EPA has responded by allowing the Water Sense program to give approval to models that have passed a performance test. We now realize that 1.6 gallons per flush is an incredible amount of fresh water to flush down a drain and as a result plenty of alternative toilet technology is now widely available. Dual flush toilets (lower volume flush for liquid, stronger volume for solids), common in European countries, are starting to become more prevalent in America. They use approximately 20 percent less than the 1.6 gallon amount required by law.

And sometimes the most obvious solutions are best. Make sure you specify a wastebasket in every bathroom. This helps to prevent the toilet from being used a wastebasket.

Dual Flush Toilets

Dual flush toilets have two buttons, one for solid and one for liquid. Since a liquid requires less force to flush, the corresponding button allows the toilet to use less water.

Kohler (*www.us.kohler.com*) is a leader in dual flush technology. They have gone thorough exhaustive testing to ensure that each toilet is as quiet as possible and has great flushing capability.

TOTO (*www.totousa.com*) practices sustainable manufacturing, engages in lifecycle assessment for their products, and even has a toilet that eliminates the need for paper.

Composting Toilets

Composting toilets have been around since the 1930s in Scandinavian countries. They require no water, are cost effective, and require less maintenance than conventional septic tank or sewer line toilet systems.

Envirolet sells attractive, low-profile, odorless systems that use organic products for waste elimination. They come in a variety of colors including a girly, hot pink. And I never thought I'd be able to use the word "girly" to describe a composting toilet.

Bio-Sun Systems (*www.best-composting-toilet.com*) toilets use no chemicals and are odorless due their forced ventilation system that accelerates waste. The waste breaks down so there is not much to clean out except mild compost every two to five years.

In a world where water is precious and scarce, this easy to install and affordable sink toilet combo by Caroman really makes a lot of sense.

Greywater Toilets

Until recently greywater in America has been considered waste, even though it is a perfectly good source for flushing toilets and irrigating landscapes. Using greywater has many benefits including reducing consumption of water, lessening the loads on municipal water systems and treatment plants, reducing energy usage, and allowing the water tables to recharge.

The Water Toilet System by Alison Norcott (*www.yankodesign.com*) is an intelligent design in which the wastewater from the shower is stored in an in-wall tank and then used to flush the toilet. To avoid bacteria growth the tank is discharged on a cyclic basis so that water isn't stored for over 24 hours. The toilet looks and functions like a gorgeous, conventional wall mounted unit.

Caroma's (*www.caromausa.com*) Profile Smart 305 won the *Popular Mechanics* Breakthrough award for 2008 and I can see why. With an attached sink that fills the tank for the next flush when you wash your hands, this space saving toilet has a dual flush feature and is easily installed.

SoCal Contractor (*www.greywaterinstaller.com*) is a construction company that specializes in green construction, including greywater systems installation. In a true green spirit the company gives a percentage of their profits to the Surfrider Foundation in an effort to help keep our oceans clean.

FAUCETS AND SHOWERHEADS

Low-flow faucets and showerheads can save a home tens of thousands of gallons of water every year. New technology in faucet aerators reduces water flow by 60 percent and typically saves three gallons of water every minute. In the bathroom, encourage homeowners to take shorter showers with faucets that have temporary turn off valves for lathering body and hair. Custom shower systems with multiple showerheads or rain panel components will probably increase water consumption. If you're going to specify these types of systems, balance out the water use by installing a greywater system for irrigating the landscape.

In order to use fewer cleaning products, specify matte plumbing fixtures instead of chrome or other shiny surfaces. The matte surface won't show as many water spots.

Installing drains in showers and tubs with baskets to catch hair can prevent clogs which will eliminate the need to flush drains with harsh chemicals.

Delta (*www.deltafaucet.com*) is a Water Sense partner working with the EPA to offer products that operate about 32 percent more efficiently than standard bathroom fixtures. Their Water Sense products help you achieve the maximum LEED points for your project. The proprietary H2OKinectic technology saves the equivalent of fifty-five bottles of water when you take an eight-minute shower. The sleek Grail and Azro faucets have proximity sensing technology. When hands come within four inches of the faucet, it turns on. It shuts off two seconds after hands are removed. Check out the green section their Web site; there's a cool LEED calculator for your water usage.

Deca (*www.deca.us.com*) sells the Aquamax rainhead that feels like a natural rainfall with full coverage spray, but boasts an eco-friendly 2.5 gpm flow rate.

Moen (*www.moen.com*) features the Envi showerhead that offers a flow rate of 1.75 gpm while increasing velocity of the water stream. No Jerry Seinfeld hair when you're done with this shower.

Evolve's (*www.evolveshowerheads.com*) Roadrunner low-flow showerhead saves about eight gallons per shower. The water trickles to almost nothing when it's fully heated, letting you know it's time to get in and wash away.

The new Wicker Park suite (*www.gerberonline.com*) has Water Sense-certified faucets and a low-flow toilet that uses only 1.8 gallons per flush.

As the winner of the 2008 EPA Water Sense Partner of the Year award, Kohler (*www.kohler.com*) has a commitment to creating water conservation products. The site hosts plenty of informative videos on water conservation and sustainable living.

Maja Ganszyniec (*www.majagan.com*) features the plugless sink—a sink that doesn't have a drain. When the washbowl is full, the user must pick up the sink and pour it down a drain. The idea here is to make the user aware of how much water they are using. Plus, there's nothing like having a super-sexy teacher—this sink is gorgeous!

WASHERS AND DRYERS

The efficiency of the washing machine has improved dramatically over the last few years. Europeans have been using front-loading machines for years, but now they are common in American homes. They use about half the water of a top-loading model because the interior does not need to be filled with water to ensure all of the fabrics will get wet. 16,000 gallons of water per household, per year can be saved per household by using front-loading washing machines. They are gentler on your clothing and use less energy to operate. The front-loading machines also spin much faster than top-loaders so more moisture is extracted from clothing, which reduces drying time. One note of caution, make sure you are ready to go once you close the door and the water begins to fill the machine. This summer my husband accidentally put his sunglasses in the wash and when we noticed, it was too late to do anything about it. The door will not open until the cycle is over because the water will spill everywhere. It resulted in a lost screw and some very clean shades.

Educate your clients about using phosphate-free and earth-friendly detergents. Some products work better than others, so run your own tests before making recommendations.

When laundry machines are installed over finished spaces, make sure there is a water collection pan to prevent water damage in the event of a burst or leaking hose.

Line dry when time and space permits—this is done is in most countries. When a dryer is used, be sure that you have specified a model with a moisture sensor. The heat turns off when the fabrics are dry, saving energy and extending the life of the fabric.

The wave of energy efficient steam washers and dryers is a breakthrough in water and energy conservation. The washers use less water than front-loading models, they run for less time, and the clothes don't end the cycle as wet, so they take even less time to dry. Not only do clothes come out cleaner and more sanitized, but they are also odor-free and less wrinkly in the steam dryer.

Both Energy Star rated Whirlpool and GE are leaders in the steam washer dryer game.

Whirlpool's Duet (*www.whirlpool.com*) received the highest rating for water efficiency, cleaning, and capacity from a leading consumer magazine. It saves 74 percent water and 80 percent energy by penetrating deep into fabric fibers,

When space is at a premium or you are saving your own energy by not having to take wet clothes out of one machine and put them in another to dry, the Fagor combo washer-dryer is the perfect little appliance.

breaking down stains like grass and grease without pre-treating. As a bonus for households with teenagers, it can wash eighteen pairs of jeans in one load.

LGL's (*www.lgl.com*) energy- and water-efficient True Steam Washer has the largest front-loading capacity machine on the market. The steam cleaning dryer leaves clothes wrinkle-free, eliminating the need for ironing. The machines have an antivibration system, so they are quiet near bedrooms.

GE's (*www.Geappliances.com*) Energy Star-rated front-load washers beat federal energy standards by 77 percent and 2007 Energy Star guidelines by up to 30 percent. The total energy and water savings can pay for the initial cost of the washer over its life.

Asko (*www.asko.com*) produces the most efficient front-load machine; it uses uses only 5.7 gallons of water.

Fagor's (*www.fagoramerica.com*) washer/dryer combo unit takes up only three cubic feet and holds thirteen pounds of laundry. It doesn't require exhaust ductwork, so it's a great solution for anywhere in a smaller footprint, eco-friendly home and wipes out the need to transfer items to the dryer.

Bosch (*www.bosch-home.com*) uses up to 76 percent less water and 72 percent less energy than conventional models.

KitchenAid (*www.kitchenaid.com*) provides some Energy Star-rated washers at more affordable prices.

Maytag (*www.maytag.com*) has reasonably priced lines with Energy Star rating.

WATER FILTERS

Installing water filters for drinking and bathing water eliminates chlorine and pesticides from the home's water supply, making the water safer and tastier. Kitchen filtration systems encourage homeowners to drink water from the tap, reducing the amount of plastic bottles that will need to be recycled or end up in landfills. Filtration systems can treat water by reverse-osmosis, ultra violet, and the well-known, least expensive, highly effective carbon filtering. Carbon filters should be replaced after three to six months of regular usage.

Aquaovo (*www.aquaovo.com*) has an eco-friendly water solution that incorporates beautiful design. The three-gallon Ovopur has a filter made of quartz, copper, activated carbon, and zinc that rids tap water of 99 percent of harmful metals.

LifeSource (*www.lifesourcewater.com*) provides entire home systems that use carbon filtering, no salt, and very little energy because the unit is powered by the water pressure. One system can last a family a lifetime.

Advanced Water Filters (*www.advancedwaterfil-*

ters.com) offers reverse osmosis and filter systems for the entire home, shower, and kitchen faucets. The site has a list of frequently asked questions to help you decide which system is best for your project.

For over a decade Miele dishwashers are my kitchen's best friend and appliance of choice. Quiet, efficient, and superbly designed machines conserve water while getting the job done right for grimey dishes or dainty crystal.

DISHWASHERS

A fully loaded dishwasher will commonly use less water than hand washing dishes, which means dishwashers are inherently the better choice for water conservation. Couple this with selecting models that use the least amount of water. All newer models use heat to wash the dishes, so select machines with booster heaters. If the homeowner is using a conventional water heater, this will allow them to set it at a lower temperature and still get the dishes sparkling clean. Maintaining the machine by clearing the food scrap basket will help the machine to operate at its highest efficiency.

Bosch (*www.bosch-home.com*) has the quietest machines in America and exceeds federal energy standards by 48 percent. The company has a corporate commitment to low-impact manufacturing and a global management system for environmental issues which maintains high standards for environmental responsibility in any place they operate.

All Miele (*www.miele.com*) products are designed to last twenty years. There is nothing better for the environment than not having to produce, transport, and dispose of products. The machines are made mostly of metal that is easier to recycle than the cast iron used in other machines. Minimal and recyclable packaging is used. The company has been financing charitable projects since 1974 and is involved in the UN Global Compact and SAI 8000 guidelines, promoting human rights, just working conditions, and environmental protection. They hold their suppliers to these same. I own a Miele dishwasher and it's the best!

In addition to being Energy Star rated, Asko (*www.asko.com*) factories have environmental certification in accordance with ISO 14001. This means that everything is done in the most environmentally friendly way possible. For example, they label for recycling all components in their appliances that weight more than fifty grams.

GE's (*www.Geappliances.com*) second generation of its Smart Dispense dishwasher is now using steam to blast baked-on particles, eliminating the need for rinsing before placing items in the dishwasher. This is an enormous leap in water savings. Other dishwashers, including my beloved Miele, claim that dishes don't need to be rinsed before you place them in the dishwasher, but anyone who has done this knows sometimes the dishes don't all come out 100 percent clean. Inevitably a few pieces end the cycle with food still on them. GE's steam cleaning actually works. In addition, it stores an entire forty-seven-ounce bottle of detergent in the machine and dispenses it as needed depending on water hardness, cycle selection, and the soil level of the dishes.

Made in the United States and competitively priced, KitchenAid (*www.kitchen-aid.com*) offers a few Energy Star rated machines.

Gaggenau (*www.gagge-nau-usa.com*) has an Energy Star certified model, DF 260/261, which provides restaurant-quality cleaning in fifty-nine minutes flat. Its Aqua Sensor technology conserves energy and water by optimizing the temperature, water quantity, and cycle length depending on the load and how badly the dishes are soiled. The automatic detergent function also adjusts to the exact amount needed, eliminating waste.

As a big consumer of produce that contains preservatives, I find myself having to make a lot of sauce out of food that would otherwise be headed for the compost bin. I was pretty excited to discover Liebherr's BioFresh system that conserves energy and helps food stay fresh longer.

DISPOSALS

The greenest kitchens won't have disposals. Instead, all food waste will be recycled in a compost pail and used as fertilizer for soil. Less water will be wasted and less garbage will have to be processed. People who practice this type of recycling tend to have less waste because they are more aware of the amount of waste they are creating. If composting is not for you, it's still better to skip the disposal and throw the food in the trash. Food sent down the drain negatively affects aquatic life and wastes electricity and about 2,000 gallons of water per year. Food waste in the trash, or the yard waste receptacle, will eventually decompose.

REFRIGERATORS

Meet or exceed Energy Star standards when you select a refrigerator. Ice or water in the door will lower your energy performance. Bottom freezers are the most efficient and side-by-side models are the least when comparing the same size refrigerators. Don't buy a larger refrigerator than is necessary. Properly clean and maintain the refrigerator to ensure optimal performance, this includes periodically vacuuming the coils.

Liebherr (*www.liebherr-appliances.com*), is the leader in green refrigerators and freezers. With a campaign they call Active Green, they were the first to become RoHS compliant and to have the least damaging effect on the environment through responsible manufacturing. They also have a separate compartment system called BioFresh. This technology provides perfect freshness for all types of food and keeps each food group at its optimum temperature and humidity so it lasts longer. This is great for organic foods, which have less preservatives. It keeps them fresh longer, resulting in less food being thrown away. This means less food in the trash and more money in your pocket.

Bosch (*www.bosch.com*) offers Energy Star rated, highly efficient models. The company has a corporate commitment to low-impact manufacturing and a global management system for environmental issues, which maintains high standards for environmental responsibility in any place they operate.

Whirlpool's new Resource Saver refrigerator (*www.whirlpool.com*) exceeds the Energy Star standard by 10 percent and uses the same energy needed to power a 60-watt bulb.

Sub-Zero (*www.subzero.com*) has been green for over sixty years. They invented dual refrigeration to keep food fresh while using less energy. Even their largest refrigerator uses less energy per month than a 100-watt light bulb. They are built in the U.S. and support organic farmers.

KitchenAid (*www.kitchenaid.com*) carries a few affordable Energy Star rated models.

Maytag (*www.maytag.com*) also carries a few affordable Energy Star rated models.

OVENS AND STOVES

In most kitchen remodels, even ones in which people don't do much cooking, a routine request is that I select a commercial-quality range. Unless someone really cooks and knows how or is willing to learn to use a commercial range, I try to talk them out of it. If you are going to specify commercial ranges, you must also specify pots and pans that will work with them. Be careful not to purchase aluminum cookware, as aluminum has been linked to

Alzheimer's disease. Teflon coated cookware is also a problem because it contains perfluorochemicals, which are carcinogenic. Clay, stainless steel, ceramic, glass, porcelain, and cast iron cookware are better choices. Also, the coatings of self-cleaning ovens become toxic when they are heated. Don't specify them.

Ovens and ranges do not have Energy Star ratings yet, but there are eco-friendly types of cooking appliance companies. Induction cooking uses much less energy than convection cooktops because all the heat goes directly to the pot instead of escaping into the room. Induction cooktops allow you to boil water in a matter of minutes so you save time and energy. The minute you remove the pot from the heat source, it is cool which is good news if you accidentally touch a burner. Jennair, Bosch, Wolf, and Viking offer induction cooktops. GE has a free-standing model with a convection oven on the bottom.

Wolf (*www.wolfappliance.com*) manufacturing plants use renewable energy, recycle, source environmentally friendly material and supplies, and provide living wages to factory workers. Made in the United States, Wolf was behaving in a green way before it became a movement.

Bosch (*www.bosch.com*) has a corporate commitment to low-impact manufacturing and a global management system for environmental issues that maintains high standards for environmental responsibility in any place they operate.

Jennair (*www.jennair.com*) combines the best elements of their cooktops with induction heating for more efficient use of energy and faster cooking times.

GE's Advantium oven (*www.Geappliances.com*) prepares meals up to eight times faster than a conventional oven while locking in moisture, and there's no need to preheat.

Viking (*www.vikingrange.com*) has married their professional performance with efficiency in their MagneQuick line. Using a preheating system and induction heating, the least amount of energy needed is used to power their cooktops and ovens.

Because of its microwave and convection qualities, the Turbo Chef oven (*www.turbochef.com*) greatly reduces cooking time. It only takes forty minutes to cook a twelve-pound turkey. The oven comes in white, stainless, and three different vibrant, two-tone color combos.

When specifying outdoor barbeques choose electric, propane, or natural gas instead of charcoal or wood briquettes.

HOODS

Using ventilation hoods while cooking helps to eliminate the indoor air pollution caused by smoke and food particles. Selecting an Energy Star rated model will help to insure that there is less noise and energy usage generated. They also feature high-performance motors and improved blade design, which provides better performance and lengthens the life of the appliance.

Zephyr (*www.zephyronline.com*) has included a new energy-efficient range hood that is Energy Star rated for its high performance ventilation and low energy consumption.

Reversomatic (*www.reversomatic.com*) is an Energy Star partner that has a line of energy-efficient ventilation products, including a kitchen range hood. In addition to meeting Energy Star performance standards, the company has an in-house air chamber where they conduct their own performance tests.

Space from Elica (*www.elica.com*) uses sound-absorbing technology to reduce 35 percent of the noise conventional hoods create. In addition to reducing noise pollution, the shape is round and radically innovative.

MICROWAVES

The reviews are mixed on microwaves. Some environmentalists say they are better than conventional cooking methods because they heat food so quickly. Other scientists say that microwaves break down the natural structure of food, making it less nutritious. When plastics and high-fat foods are cooked in the microwave, dioxin is released into the food and, ultimately, into our bodies. I remember when the microwave first showed up at my house. I was ten. Even then, I suspected that it wasn't all that healthy. Years later a friend's dad pulled out a gigameter, placed it next to the microwave, and the radiation measurement was going ballistic. That was enough to keep them out of my house forever. I've been told repeatedly that today's models are safer and sealed, so buy at your own risk. Another reason I stay microwave-free is for weight control. When you have to pull out a pot and reheat something, it takes time and effort. You really have to be hungry to go through that routine! If you're going to install a microwave, select a new model. All newer microwave heating is more efficient.

VACUUMS

Vacuuming once daily is one of the most effective and easy ways to improve indoor air quality and prevent allergies. You would be amazed at the amount of dust that accumulates on a floor in a 24-hour period. In addition to human and pet skin and hair, fine particles from rugs, furniture, window treatments, and other surfaces end up in the air and eventually on the floors as the items break down over time.

Electrolux UltraSilencer vacuums (*www.electrolux-usa.com*) are equipped with a high-efficiency suction fan and bare floor nozzle, and clean up with noticeably less

Here's a vacuum that will last forever and won't wake up napping little ones. For exhausted parents, this may be the best vacuum money can buy. For the rugrat-less crowd, you'll equally love this vaccum. It cleans like nobody's business.

noise. The energy-saving vacuum is made of 55 percent recycled plastic with a good portion recycled from cars. The packaging contains 80 percent recycled and unbleached cardboard and the manuals are printed on recycled paper. Priced under $300, this vacuum packs a lot of value for the cost.

Bosch (*www.bosch-home.com*) has a premium vacuum that is eco-friendly, high-performance and comes at a range of affordable price points. They have HEPA filters and a zero-emissions sealed body, which is especially good for an allergy sufferer. Plus they suck really well.

Miele's Earth HEPA vacuum (*www.mieleusa.com*) is an energy-conserving machine that automatically adjusts to the power level needed for the surface being cleaned. The sealed system and active HEPA captures and retains tiny, lung-damaging particles including dust mites and pollen and also absorbs odors. At nearly a thousand dollars, it's not cheap, but like most Miele products, which I love so much, it is extremely quiet and lasts and lasts.

The Roomba vacuum robot (*www.irobot.com*) has changed my life. As a person with an undiagnosed case of OCCD (obsessive compulsive cleaning disorder), I spent at least fifteen minutes each day sweeping and vacuuming. Seemingly too good be true, the Roomba travels around the entire house or office all day long picking up anything that isn't nailed down. It's powerful and goes effortlessly from hard surfaces to plush carpet. If you like a clean floor, make the investment. Check in with Costco, they sell the Roomba for about $100 less than anyplace else.

DEHUMIDIFIERS

Dehumidifiers absorb excess moisture in the air, which can cause mold and mildew. Chose an Energy Star rated model that has enough capacity to run in the desired space. Most dehumidifiers have an automatic shut-off valve to prevent overflowing when the water tray becomes full; make sure yours does too. This helps to avoid accidental flooding. Some models have hoses that drain the water into a specified area. This eliminates having to carry heavy buckets of water through the interior. Also important is the selection of a model that has a built in humidistat, a device which allows you set the desired temperature for the room or home. The machine turns off when this temperature is reached. If the entire home needs

to be dehumidified, there are whole home models.

Quality Matters (*www.qualitymatters.com*) sells the Danby dehumidifier line, which features Energy Star rating, portability, automatic shut-off, and a direct vent option.

Air & Water (*www.air-n-water.com*) offers the Alen MDF3-50 portable model. Energy Star rated, this unit holds fifty pints of water, and has a humidistat and two fan speeds.

HOME BRAINS

Smart home automation systems allow you to control music, movies, lights, temperature, landscape irrigation, and security systems from anywhere in your home or the world. By organizing the systems of the home to work together, you not only gain control over these systems, but also conserve energy. Room temperatures are regulated with in-home key pads or remotely, and the systems even automate shades to open and close with the sunlight, reducing the work the climate control system has to do. Indoor and exterior lighting are controlled with programmable timers, dimmers, and motion sensors for the highest efficiency. Audio-visual media uses power sensing wireless outlet switches, which eliminate the need for power hungry standby modes by cutting power to A/V devices when they are not in use. Even the security systems can be integrated with the rest of the home. At the time of writing this book there are several companies researching smart home automation, which integrates regulation and storage of residential, renewable energy systems. Keep your eyes open; this is the future of green design.

Control4 (*www.Control4.com*) has an affordable, scalable system which operates efficiently, regulating HVAC, lights, spa, pool pumps, sprinklers, and even alerting you via e-mail in the event of a water leak, fire, or security breach. With access screens that can be viewed throughout the home or via the Internet, Control4 provides a homeowner peace of mind while respecting the planet. Brochures are printed on recycled materials.

Somfy's products (*www.somfysystems.com/*)have the ability to be operated by a PC or a handheld device, and provide end users with the ability to enhance their control over motorized window coverings and lighting while assisting in the conservation of energy.

The Energy Management system from Vantage (*www.vantagecontrols.com*) provides consumers with an end-to-end solution, including measuring current usage, which allows immediate changes in consumption and provides real-time feedback on actual cost savings. At the touch of button, the system can dim the lights, turn off appliances, and adjust temperature. The system also offers up-to-date weather conditions, which help save water

7 LIVING ROOMS

when adjusting sprinklers to outdoor climate conditions. After reading chapters 2 through 6 you have the essential ingredients to make your design project green. The next step is to combine these pieces in a sustainable manner. Your success in accomplishing an environmentally friendly space will be the result of careful thinking about how to assemble these materials and furnishings and how space is used. The design of an eco-friendly home relies heavily on the concepts of creatively using all of its living spaces, including the outdoors, and doing more with less. It requires a completely different approach toward possessions and dwellings that places more value on quality than quantity.

For the last twenty years I've paid close attention to the way European city dwellers live. Everything is compact; they have fewer things, yet they live very elegant, well-appointed lives. Conversely, many North Americans have rooms that are rarely used, yards that are frequently deserted, and a lot of things they don't need or use, but continue to store, wasting valuable space and energy to maintain. By building smaller dwellings with cleverly utilized spaces, filling them with possessions that are truly important to a lifestyle, and taking advantage of outdoor areas, whether a private yard or a public park, you can truly maximize your "living rooms" while simultaneously saving resources, energy, and pollution.

BUILDING SMALL

One of the most common questions I hear pertaining to a green project is, "How much will it cost me to go green?" Knowing what I know, it's easy to reply with, "How much will it cost you if you don't go green?" This book has illustrated, chapter after chapter, how wasteful behavior costs us more than money. It literally threatens our health and future generations' existence on our magnificent planet. I like to look at the glass as half full in my life experiences and the current economic downturn is no exception. It has forced us to revisit the lessons of conservation taught to us by our parents and grandparents. This

responsible way of thinking has resulted in an interest in smaller, healthier, well-built, energy-efficient homes. In the past few months I've seen more than one headline discussing the death of the McMansion. Thankfully, we are now seeing the principles of sustainability becoming mainstream and an increase in behavior that values sensibility over excess. Showing off how much we have is simply out of style.

The fact is that the average family size has been declining for thirty-five years. We just don't need such big homes anymore. Finally, we are starting to see a shift in our culture of returning to what makes sense. According to *USA Today*, new homes, after doubling in size since 1960, are shrinking for the first time in decades. The average square footage of single-family homes has fallen from 2,629 to 2,343. With the focus on less square footage, an emphasis on good design with regard for our future becomes imperative.

So the lesson is to build as small as you can, because smaller homes are simply more efficient. They use less energy and raw materials to build and produce considerably less construction site waste. Once they're up and running they take less energy to clean, heat, cool, and furnish. Additionally less square footage amounts to lower labor and material costs. So an added bonus of building smaller is that you have a larger percentage of the budget to spend on quality materials that add value to the home and your portfolio. Building small also inspires innovative solutions to design problems resulting in more unique and interesting living spaces. Even retailers are paying attention to the trend of smaller homes. Stores like Crate and Barrel and Cisco Brothers have begun carrying smaller-scaled lines of furniture and appliance manufacturer Fagor is selling more of its combo washer/dryer units than ever before.

An additional benefit to smaller homes is a feeling of connectedness to a community. People with less private interior spaces tend to take advantage of what the community has to offer. Libraries, parks, swimming pools, civic centers, coffee shops, and museums offer opportunities to come into contact with your neighbors. Most of this book was written in a public library. Even in an enormous metropolis like Los Angeles, I find myself running into my new library friends all over the city. It makes the city a whole lot smaller when you see smiling faces you recognize. Plus, when you're out, you're using less energy in your individual home and, instead, are sharing the same resources with many.

This long and narrow dining room is the result of removing an outdated and never used wet bar area and transforming it into a truly useable space. A backless bench is pushed against one wall and a sofa the client already owned is placed against the other wall. Entry is available from either side of the room. An oversized floor mirror rests against the far wall to reflect the good times and make the room seem more spacious. The light-filled space is also a cozy area for curling up with a book.

Great room by Lori Dennis, photo by Ken Hayden

This open space accommodates a variety of activities allowing cooking, entertaining, and lounging to occur simultaneously. There's enough room for people to feel like they aren't on top of each other. I installed mirrors to make the space feel even roomier.

ELIMINATING "STUFF"

The easiest way to gain square footage for living space is to get rid of things you don't need or use. Good organization of important, necessary items is the key to being able to live in smaller spaces. The main reason we think we need so much space is because we have too much stuff. My favorite design show on television was the one where they cleaned out the all of the junk in houses by putting the items out in the yard in piles labeled keep, throw away, sell, donate. I was thrilled to see that without spending a dime or using any new resources these homeowners discovered hundreds of extra square footage. I witnessed this first hand after my

friends, a married couple with a nine-year-old daughter, complained for years about how they had no space and needed to move to a bigger home. It never made any sense to me because they were only three people who lived in what I considered a generously sized home (2,000 square feet) with three bedrooms, three bathrooms, a formal living and dining space, and a family room. This year they bit the bullet and had a huge yard sale. Over a couple of hours they made a few thousand dollars, visited with their neighbors, and discovered that they really did have quite a bit of space.

If you have items that you aren't using, give them away, donate them to a charity, or sell them. Don't allow them to become old, damaged, and eventually useless. This reminds me of deteriorating cars I see parked on the street or in people's driveways. I always wonder why someone didn't just put them up for sale or donate them instead of letting them rot away and become eyesores.

Incorporating sliding doors into an open floorplan allows flexibility for public and private spaces.

When you get something new, get rid of the old thing it replaced. This is especially useful with clothing. If you haven't worn an item in a year, you probably never will again.

Unless you truly love something for its aesthetic value or it really serves a purpose, seriously consider getting rid of it. Not only will you gain space, but you will also have less to clean and maintain. So you gain time and money by saying bye-bye to clutter.

OPEN FLOORPLANS

We've been building homes the same way for the last 100 years by separating spaces for individual uses. The fact that this isn't working for modern life is validated by the popularity of the great room over the last decade and the recent flood of live-work loft spaces. In shelter magazines, for sale listings, on home and improvement shows—everywhere I look it seems that live-work loft spaces are front and center. Ironically, these wide-open, multipurpose spaces actually bring us full circle from the times when all living was done in one space. Think igloos, teepees, and cabins with potbelly stoves.

Half the battle is already won—because people are embracing these new configurations of space, you won't need to convince them to forgo their walls. However, it requires a shift in traditional space-planning skills, especially when you are limited in square footage. It becomes essential

to lose the idea of individual spaces for kitchen, dining, living room and the den. Instead, design a "great space" which meets the needs of all of the public living areas. The popular loft style embodies these very principles. In these configurations, single, well thought out rooms keep occupants connected, while allowing them to perform individual tasks. But because so many activities are occurring in one space, it is crucial to install furniture and durable materials, which are easy to clean and contain plenty of clever storage options.

Doing most of your living in one main area does fit a lot of life into less square footage, but there are also issues of privacy and noise that must be addressed. One of the most successful ways to create quiet, private spaces is to incorporate sliding doors, which act as temporary room dividers, into your plans. Simply open or close them to accommodate different activities. Plants, rugs, and fabric on furniture or window treatments also help to absorb sound.

MULTIPURPOSE SPACES

Whether or not you choose an open floorplan, designing green challenges you to work on plans where spaces have multiple functions. Instead of immediately turning to the solution of adding square footage when more space is required, you must brainstorm how you can repurpose rooms that are rarely used like formal living rooms and dining rooms.

Some of the most charming dining rooms I've seen have doubled as libraries, which inspired me to use this technique in my own projects. Most formal dining rooms, used only a few times a year, are a wonderful place to do things like plan menus, do homework, work on projects, and research. A dining room with extra-deep banquettes can be used for additional sleeping quarters in its off hours. Something as simple as placing a sofa on at least one side of the table makes the room feel like you're in a boutique hotel lounge and provides a perfect spot to curl up with a book when other areas of the home are occupied with noisier activities. This furniture arrangement works well in any style interior.

Rarely used formal living rooms are another great way to recapture space. Instead of waiting to enter this area only when special guests arrive, consider using it as a small home office or a multimedia or music room. The growing trend in home offices has resulted in manufacturers designing attractive furniture with plenty of storage space that blends in with other living spaces. Since armoires are rarely used for televisions anymore with the popularity of the flat screen, a similar-sized piece of furniture, like a secretary, will be in scale in a living room while secretly housing a computer, files, an all-in-one fax

Dining room by Lori Dennis, photo by Mark Tanner

The shelves in this dining room house a rather large collection of cookbooks owned by a chef. The table does double duty as an area to map out meals and serves as a dining or buffet surface. Being in this space is a delight to the senses as you scan the titles for every imaginable type of cuisine and then enjoy tasting them too.

machine, printer, copier, and scanner, and office supplies. A beautiful desk and bookshelves can be incorporated into any space, even the most formal of designs. The seating already present in living room design accommodates any guests that may visit "the office." I don't know about you, but I much prefer to work in room filled with natural light and sensational furnishings than a commercial-looking office.

Formal living rooms also double nicely as music rooms. Whether it was coming from musical instruments, radios, or recordings, listening to music in the living room was a popular activity before televisions arrived. It's still a civilized way to use space. Create attractive displays for instruments and hidden storage for less attractive items like music books, gaming consoles, CDs, and LPs. Even if you don't actually play an instrument, video games like Rock Band and Guitar Hero allow anyone to enjoy the sensation. Using the living room as a place to enjoy music adds life to the space and allows the space to live up to its name.

Consider using a hallway as a mini gallery or for coat or purse storage. Displaying a collection of sculptures, paintings, or photographs in the same manner as a museum makes traveling through any hall an entertaining experience. Placing hooks along a hall for coats and purses helps to alleviate the need for more closet storage and reminds you of all the stylish choices which may have been forgotten had they been stashed in a closet.

In a kitchen, remove cabinet doors to make room for a cookbook collection or easy access to cooking items, and to give the room an extra few feet of visual space. This is very helpful in a small kitchen where more than one person is cooking or serving. I just watched *Julie and Julia*, a movie about Julia Child. In addition to inspiring my husband and me to try some new recipes, I felt great about our small kitchen. Julia, truly one of the most well-known and beloved chefs of the twentieth century, made magic every day in a tiny kitchen. Adopting European inspiration, she made efficient use of every spot. Her pots lined the walls on pegboard and, with the addition of place mats and fine china, the table transformed from prep area to dining in minutes.

Installing a soft banquette next to the farmhouse dining table serves two purposes. First, it allows the maximum number of diners to enjoy meals in this relatively small space. Second, it easily transforms into a comfortable area for afternoon naps or overnight guests.

While you may recognize the value of designing for and living in less space you're probably wondering how you are going to fit the furniture necessary for so many functions into a smaller space. You do it by designing multi-tasking furniture pieces. For example, a dining table that lives behind the sofa can serve three purposes: a wider version of a console table with lighting, a desk during the day, and a dining table at night. You can pull it away from the back of the sofa and even add leaves when you need to accommodate more people. Tables with shelves under them can be good hidden storage by placing a floor length tablecloth on them. This is also a great way to change up a look. One of my favorites is using a long, low (20-inch) bookshelf with cushions for seating on the ends and a television stand in the middle. I put baskets in the shelves containing packing supplies, throws, books, and baby toys. That way I can watch my daughter play or

Dining room by Lori Dennis, photo by Mark Tanner

Whether your style is modern or leans toward the traditional, you can use a chic secretary to hide unsightly office equipment in your living/work space.

nap, hang out with my husband while he's watching the news, wrap a package that needs to be shipped, and have extra seating when a full house has arrived.

While Ikea may not be a place where you want to shop, they are experts in the multipurpose room category. If you're ever near one, plan a visit to the store. Once you are inspired by the genius of their space planning, you can substitute higher-end materials and furniture using the same compact solutions.

A final consideration in multipurpose spaces is that the lighting needs to be adaptable for each use. Even the most well-designed room will go flat without proper lighting. For example, a dining room that also serves as a library will require varied amounts of lights, as will a living room that doubles as an office or music room. Of course it's always best to have as much natural light as possible throughout the day. For night plan on a variety of lighting fixtures including recessed lighting, cove lighting, sconces, and table and floor lamps. They should all be on energy efficient dimmers to accommodate the individual "moods" desired in these spaces.

REORGANIZING FOR REUSE

Before you buy anything, try to reuse what you own. It's one of the most basic and least expensive ways to go green. Doing this has no environmental impact and saves you money for other parts of the project. It almost sounds like it's too easy of a solution, but it really works.

Last weekend my firm shot photos of a client's project. During photo shoots it is routine to move things around to new places to accommodate the camera's view. I always find that at least one of the changes turns out to be for the better and leave the new arrangement intact

You don't have to have a lot of money or time to make the most of an older kitchen design. In this kitchen, the doors were removed and painted with an eco-friendly, celadon paint. Having open shelves added a few feet of visual space to the kitchen, allowing more than one person to work in the kitchen and really making it easier to find items. One thing to remember about this design is that you have to be organized and neat with exposed shelves.

after the camera is long gone. In this particular project, when it came time to buy furniture for the home, the 2008 recession had hit my client especially hard (he's in real estate). He was pretty glum about the fact that there was no money left for new furniture. We didn't even have a budget for recovering old items. Fortunately, I find this type of challenge exhilarating. Where he saw a problem, I knew there was a great big, green solution.

The two key areas that were problematic were the living room, with its mismatched, temporary furnishings and a missing sofa, and the entry hall, which felt empty without any furniture. The client planned to recover financially and then purchase a new sofa and fabric to reupholster existing chairs in the living room and a round, wood table in the entry. I walked around the home looking for solutions and discovered that if I switched out the two problem chairs in the living room for his off-white sofa and chairs in the master retreat, the living room would

For those who never seem to have enough closet space, install hooks in a corridor or on a bathroom wall and hang your purses, belts, and hats. Using the space under a staircase isn't a new idea, but placing something chic in it, like the wine cellar on page 74, is one of the best design ideas I've ever seen.

Wine cellar by Nicole Sassaman, photo by Cole Sassaman

Living room by Lori Dennis, photo by Ken Hayden

come together nicely with only a few accent pillows. Inspired by this success, I located a console table in a long hallway, repositioned it under a painting in a corner of the entry, and saw that it worked even better than the round, center table idea. I replaced the hall console with an appropriately scaled bench I found buried in storage. The photographer was amazed, the client couldn't stop thanking me, and I got the shots I wanted without spending a dime or using any new resources. This is a seven-million-dollar, Old World Italianate home. If this type of "working it out" will suffice in the high-end of traditional, it will certainly work in more flexible and forgiving styles, too. Professionals who charge markups may want to rethink their compensation and bill by the hour or

The console table in this photo was being used in another part of the home. It was entirely too big for that space and resulted in an area that was crowded and difficult to pass through. By simply rethinking our plan to buy a predictable round entry table, we were able to give the console a home that fit perfectly.

quote flat fees for each project. Being paid for creative solutions is far more rewarding and environmentally responsible than being a good salesperson and getting clients to buy unnecessary things.

AVOID HIGH CURRENTS

Pay very close attention to where you place service panels and high-current wiring runs. They should be kept as far as possible from heavily used interior spaces, especially bedrooms.

No one would ever know that these pieces of furniture were "found" in other areas of the home and relocated to the living room. By adding a few throw pillows and grounding with a rug, the room looked completely finished without the client buying one new piece of furniture.

GET SOME FRESH AIR, IT'S GOOD FOR YOU

As you build with sensitivity to the environment you gain a connection to the outdoor elements like fresh air, natural light, plants, and wildlife. Outdoor spaces can range from edible gardens, wood deck patios, stone-covered sitting areas, commercial kitchens, delightful trails—the list is endless. Good green design will allow you to add usable square footage to a home by expanding living spaces to the exterior, while using the least amount of materials and energy possible. Currently most Americans spend 90 percent of our time indoors although being outside is part of the human experience and so much better for us (when conditions permit). The air quality is better outside and vitamin D production from sun exposure actually helps ward off sickness. I recently attended a lecture where Mariel Hemingway spoke about sustainable practices to

Photo by Roi Yerushalmi

You know the song, "Nobody walks in LA." Sadly, it's kind of true. It makes meeting neighbors difficult when they go from garage to car and then on their way. Here I am capitalizing on a rare opportunity to meet my neighbors while strolling with my baby. Thankfully these front yard gardens are popping up all over the city. Not only do they promote healthy living, less pollution, and a sense of community, they are really quite beautiful.

Landscape architecture by Jaime Gibbs, photos by Cliff Chilluffo

help people slow down and de-stress. Her best advice was to enjoy outdoor spaces. Long before there was artificial air conditioning people sat and slept outside on porches, saying hi to neighbors as they passed and breathing fresh air. Well-designed outdoor spaces will encourage people to get back outside and return to healthier lifestyles. This advice isn't new, but it's still good and bears repeating.

HOW SPACE IS USED

Really think about how the space will be used. Is it a place for entertaining, relaxing, gardening, sports, pets, a playground for children, or all of the above? Is there insufficient space inside? Will the outdoors relieve interior space concerns? What are the views you want to see

On the grounds of this east coast estate, cut flower patches were strategically planted along walking paths. The owners and their guests enjoy the vibrant colors and sweet-smelling fragrances as they stroll the grounds. And the flowers, in close proximity to paths, are easy to reach for cutting. Indigenous varieties of flowers were selected for the region's soil and climate. This allows optimal growing and eliminates the need for irrigation, fertilizer, or pesticides.

from the interior? From the exterior? How will the indoor and outdoor spaces relate to each other? How can you utilize the outdoors in most types of weather? Does the space need to be protected from sun, pollution, or noise? How can you include landscaping that drains properly and minimizes outdoor water consumption or harmful maintenance chemicals?

You must also take into consideration what is already there and how to preserve natural conditions. Ask yourself the following questions. How do you protect existing trees, vegetation, and natural habitats? How will the current interior lighting affect the exterior moods? How do you maintain soil retention? Are there current natural or manmade structures which can be incorporated into the design?

Only when you have answers to these types of questions should you begin making an exterior plan.

KILL YOUR LAWN

Frequently, large areas of grass—lawns—are default solutions to exterior space planning. When you really think about the concept of maintaining a conventional lawn, it begins to make less and less sense to have one.

Traditional lawns require an enormous amount of maintenance, which creates various environmental burdens.

Edible garden by Barbara Treves, photo by Derek Rath

In this backyard, water isn't wasted on a blanket of grass. Intelligently designed drip systems conserve water when they irrigate the raised planters. Edible herbs and veggies add color and texture to the space and provide the owners with fabulous tasting meals.

In order for a lawn to be lush and green it typically requires regular applications of fertilizers and pesticides. When the rain comes, these chemicals run off into sewers, which require treatment or, worse, pollute waterways. In many parts of North America lawns need to be artificially irrigated which places unnecessary strains on fresh water supplies. The thing I find most absurd about lawns in the constant desire to make them grow only to have to cut and trim them weekly. Adding to the offenses, gas-operated mowers, trimmers, and weed whackers emit noxious fumes and pollution. Replacing a lawn with indigenous plants, edible gardens, permeable paving, or wildlife habits will create a significant decline in the amount toxic runoff, wasted energy, and pollution. It will also save a homeowner a tremendous amount of man-hours and money in the long run.

If there is already a significant lawn in place, there will be considerable costs to remove and replace it with another solution. This cost is typically lower, however, in comparison to the cost of maintaining a lawn.

If you just can't do without the lawn, try to install only the maximum amount needed for dogs or children. Plant native turf grasses or wild grasses, which are more drought tolerant, potentially fire resistant, and require fewer fertilizers and pesticides and less maintenance.

Artificial turf is also an option. Companies like *Synlawn.com* and *Easyturf.com* supply realistic looking synthetic grass that requires little maintenance and no water or chemicals.

NATIVE PLANTS AND WILDLIFE

Planting indigenous, regional plants requires a lot less environmental burden. These types of plants tend to need little, if any, chemical pesticides or herbicides because they have adapted to their climate and soil conditions. The occasional addition of compost and beneficial insects is about the only booster shot needed for native plants to flourish. When planting, consider species that contain berries, flowers (nectar), and seeds as they will encourage wildlife like butterflies, honeybees, and hummingbirds to visit the garden. Unless you have visited such a place, you cannot imagine the peaceful feeling you get from seeing these little creatures buzz around.

Native flower varieties can also be planted in cutting gardens as a simple, convenient solution to buying chemical-laden, store-bought flowers. Pollinated and fragrant species will penetrate indoor living areas so be sure to ask the homeowner about any plant allergies.

EDIBLE GARDENS

I live in a city where ordinary homes sell for up to $2,600 per square foot. Space is really at a premium, even for the wealthy. When I walk around and see the amount of square footage dedicated to front yards, which I never see people using, I am amazed. Most front yards are planted with grass, which makes no sense in a desert climate where water is scarce. Even in climates with plenty of rainfall, lawns still waste so much energy, time, and toxins constantly trying to grow grass, keep it free from weeds, and then cutting it. I walk nearly every evening and imagine a time when people just let the grass die and plant edible and cut flower gardens. With Los Angeles' water shortage and the national increases in the prices of water and food, that time might not be so far away.

Although we tend to think of a residential yard as a private space, the yard can really be an opportunity to create a more tightly knit sense of community by opening it up and using it. The idea that more people will get outside and garden in the front yard is entirely plausible, especially in light of the interest in organic food. For a short time in my life I was lucky to live in a small town in Pennsylvania where people sat on their front porches or worked in their flower gardens. When you walked down the street, you interacted with your neighbors. There was a community. It is a stark contrast to the city in which I live now, where many of us have no idea who lives literally next door. The good news is that I'm starting to see front yard gardens pop up in Los Angeles. There are people (actual owners not gardeners) working in them and folks passing by now, stopping to say, "Hello, what a pretty garden." So far I've spotted three in my neighborhood. It inspired me to plant my own vegetable garden in the tiny patch of soil outside of my home. In about a week I will be enjoying my first urban garden-grown tomato. I've heard it said that picking and eating your own vegetables is a true luxury like eating caviar. Well, I do love caviar so I can't wait for this tomato.

In fact, the edible garden topic has popped up all over the Internet and in news stories. Following Michelle Obama's lead at the White House, seven million Americans are predicted by the National Gardening Association to start their own vegetable gardens this year. Even urban dwellers are growing their own lettuce, tomatoes, and peas in pots on rooftops, in sun-filled spaces, and in front yards. If you're an organic produce eater like me, it is the freshest, most nutritious food you will ever eat. Plus, the time you spend gardening gets you outside, which means you're not using the interior utilities. The big bonus for the environment is that the food you grow doesn't cause any pollution in transportation. I also tend to believe that someone who is going to eat their own produce may be a bit less liberal with the toxic chemicals on it.

And P.S., if you are planting an herb garden, make sure it is close to the kitchen so the herbs will be readily available when you need them.

LIGHTING

If you live in the country, you have a pleasure most urban and suburban folks do not get to enjoy each evening: a view of the stars. Until I took the LEED exam, I did not even know that light "pollution" has negative effects other than not being able to see stars. The light that escapes from our buildings and exterior landscapes alters human sleep patterns, plant growth, and wildlife behavior.

To help combat the problem, install energy-efficient lighting with motion sensors that have fixtures to prevent light from exiting out above the fixture. The International Dark Sky Association actually provides a manufacturer's directory with a list of approved light fixtures (*www.darksky.org*).

NOISE POLLUTION

If an outdoor space is to flow with the interiors, in addition to being aesthetically pleasing and functioning well it must be protected from unwanted noise. It's nearly impossible to create an indoor-outdoor flow, or even keep windows open, when you hear unpleasant noises outside, like vehicles, other people, helicopters, and barking dogs. The two best ways I know to combat exterior noise are running water and massive amounts of plants, trees, or shrubs.

Exterior fountains and ponds are also noisy, but the sound the water makes is a pleasant one for most people. Fountains and ponds with small waterfalls incorporated between the noise and living areas will help to create a more peaceful environment. They may also attract small animals looking for water, so plan accordingly.

Lush trees, hedges, shrubs, and vines planted on the border of a property also serve to diminish unwanted noise. The thicker the planting, the more noise will be blocked. Additionally trees, hedges, shrubs, and vines provide privacy, security, and safety.

OUTDOOR KITCHENS

Whenever possible, include an outdoor area for cooking. There must be something in our DNA that attracts us to places where food is cooking. Most parties wind up in the kitchen and an outdoor "kitchen" is no exception. Preparing and grilling food outside has three primary benefits. First, since most people cook outside when it is warm, doing so saves energy and reduces the burden on the utilities when air conditioning loads are probably highest. Second, there is always less clean up when food is prepared on a grill. Less clean up means you use less water, energy, and other resources. Third, food takes on a whole new flavor and feel when it is prepared (and hopefully eaten) outside. The variety in dining experience brought on by a cookout seems to make people really happy.

FINALLY...

After you have put what you learn into practice and have designed an eco-friendly interior you will also be responsible for encouraging your clients to change their behaviors in ways that will reduce energy and create healthier homes. Teaching them practices like water conservation, using ceiling fans in conjunction with good airflow instead of turning on the air conditioning, turning down the thermostat in the winter because you've ensured that the building has been properly insulated and windows and doors are sealed for efficiency, turning off lights when leaving a room or using natural light during the day, wiping feet off on a mat or simply removing shoes before entering a home, and cleaning with environmentally friendly products will enable them to participate in an energy-efficient and healthy lifestyle while enjoying the environment you have helped to create.

8 BEDROOMS AND NURSERIES

Even the most experienced practitioner will find it nearly impossible to make a home completely green. Some factors pertaining to building or remodeling structures are simply out of your control. You have even less control over your environment when you go to work, the gym, shopping, or travelling. There is one area of the home, however, in which you can take control by concentrating your green efforts: the bedroom. Since most of us spend a third of our lives in the bedroom of our home, it makes sense to to make it the greenest and healthiest room of the home. The eight hours we spend sleeping each night is a vunerable time for our bodies to literally regenerate. When you sleep your brain is creating hormones like melatonin which help to fight diseases. A space that has clean air, plenty of sunlight during the day and darkness during the night, nontoxic furniture, environmentally sound materials, and a void of hazardous electromagnetic fields gives the body the best chance to recuperate from the debilatating poisons we encounter on a daily basis.

A nontoxic bedroom is even more crucial for infants and children who pound for pound are much more susceptible to the dangerous chemicals found in most conventional furniture, fabrics, and finish materials. Unfortunately, most parents don't realize this when they set up nurseries for a newborn (or decorate spaces for their children). With the best intentions, they rush out and purchase new flooring, paint, furniture, accessories, toys, mattresses, and linens. If the materials aren't green, chances are the room is flooded with toxic offgases. To make matters worse, parents often close all the windows so the child won't "catch a draft." It's a perfect storm of chemicals inundating the infant or child who has an already compromised immune system. I will never forget when I visited my girlfriend's new home. She had just painted the entire house, including her 6-week-old baby's new nursery. It was obvious that she hadn't paid attention to my green decorating advice when I walked in the door and the fumes almost made me fall down. She proudly turned to me and said, "Don't you just love that new paint smell?" I shook my head and told her to open all the windows and get the fans going immediately.

WALL AND CEILING MATERIALS

All surface materials should be nontoxic. Use no-VOC paints, healthy wall covering, or earth plaster. None of these products should release harmful chemicals into the bedroom or nursery.

This serene space invites you to a sound sleep, especially when the mattress is made of latex and organic wool toppers.

If humidity levels are a concern, consider breathable surfaces like earth plaster for its ability to absorb and release moisture as needed. Regulating the humidity levels will also reduce the need for a humidifier, which could present its own health problems. Unless the water cartridges of humidifiers are routinely cleaned with peroxide, they are breeding grounds for microbial growth. When you combine dirty humidifiers with carpets or rugs and closed windows you are certain to have a proliferation of bacterial growth.

Contrary to popular opinion, you should keep humidifiers out of infant rooms.

FRESH AIR AND NATURAL LIGHT

Bedrooms should have operable windows that allow plenty of air and natural light into the room. Even in the colder months, fresh air needs to circulate in a room. Especially in an infant's room, there needs to be an abundance of oxygen. If it is sealed tight, the baby will breathe in the oxygen all night until there isn't much left. This is not an optimal condition for brain development. Ceiling fans in conjunction with open windows really aid in bringing air circulation into the space. UV rays from the sun act as a natural disinfectant. So at least once daily open the windows and window coverings to allow the elements to come in and the toxins to leave.

ELECTRONICS

Less is more in a bedroom. Bau-biologists believe that electromagnetic fields (EMFs) can compromise human health. EMFs are manmade radiation from manmade electrical current. The AC current comes from electronics, like clocks and televisions, and the DC current occurs when metal, like the coils in conventional boxsprings, become magnetized. An actual measurable low level of electrical current is stored, concentrated, and radiates from the metal coils and throws off the human body's own natural, magnetic field. It affects our cells' ability to communicate with each other and can cause changes in functions of cells and tissues. It does sound a little sci-fi, but when you wake from a night of tossing and turning, feeling fatigued, it may well be the EMFs negatively affecting you. More serious side effects include: decreases in melatonin, alterations of the immune system, accelerated tumor growth, changes in biorhythms, and changes in brain activity and heart rate.

Bedroom by Lori Dennis, photo by Mark Tanner

There are two ways to reduce the problem: remove electronics from the bedroom and do not sleep in beds or mattresses which contain metal. Choose battery operated alarm clocks, sound machines, and any other device that is close to your head. Do not locate a home office in the bedroom. Keep cell phone chargers, fax machines, printers and computers out of the bedroom. As crazy as it sounds, televisions should not be in bedrooms either. Steer clear of electric blankets by dressing warmer or adding more blankets. In an infant's room remove the monitor from the crib and place it at least three feet from the baby on the dresser. They will still effectively pick up sound.

BEDROOM FURNISHINGS

Bedrooms often become repositories for "stuff" like books, magazines, medications, boxes, and clothing. Clean it out. A clutter-free bedroom is mandatory for a relaxing, meditative space.

Closets are generally located in or near bedrooms. If you bring dry-cleaned clothes into the home, remove plastic and air them out near an open window. Or, even better, use an eco-friendly dry cleaner. Wearing, sleeping in or near, or breathing conventionally dry-cleaned items can increase your chances for getting cancer.

MATTRESSES, PILLOWS, AND TOPPERS

Select natural fiber pillows and mattresses. Most mattresses are treated with a fire retardant chemical like polybrominated diphenyl ethers (PBDEs). This carcinogen acculumlates in humans who are exposed to it and can cause breast cancer and irregular brain development in children. Replace commercial mattresses with natural fiber mattresses. Chemical-free wool is a natural fire retardant that won't harm you.

Most foam pillows are sprayed with flame retardants known to cause irreversable damage to children's nervous systems. Unless otherwise stated, foam is generally made from petrochemicals which offgas chemicals throughout the night, right into your face, mouth, nose, throat, and skin. Synthetic pillows also have a higher percentage of dust mites found in the dense coarse foam material. Down or feather pillows, sometimes believed to cause allergies, are actually better solutions as the tightly woven fabric used to contain feathers and down acts as a barrier to keep dust mites out of the pillow.

Human beings sweat during the night, about a pint per night on average. This is a natural way to release toxins in the body. But these fluids go right into the pillow and mattress. The trapped moisture, chemicals, fire retardants, and poly foam materials are a conducive environment for

Conventional thinking has been that a child's room should be sealed up tight so they don't "catch a draft" and get sick, when actually an infant or child's room should be flooded with fresh air and light. The UV rays act as a disinfectant, the air is able to circulate and natural light creates a far superior environment for playing, reading, or resting.

microbial growth and dust mites. Protect pillows, mattresses, duvets, and blankets with natural fiber covers that can be washed regularly. Wool mattress toppers covered in organic cotton wick away moisture and can be washed easily and regularly.

In infant rooms it is especially important to buy organic fiber mattress pads and mattresses with no metal coils. First, doing so eliminates low level fields of electric radiation. Second, throw up, urine, and drool combines with the plastic of commercial mattresses and creates super-charged bacteria. Underdeveloped immune and endocrine systems are compromised in this situation. Recently, studies have supported the belief that SIDS is a side effect of a toxic mattress. For the same reason, mattresses shouldn't be stored in the garage. Carbon monoxide from car exhaust concentrates in mattresses which can poison an infant when they breathe the fumes. To keep a

In these children's rooms, the designer relied on eco-friendly, no-VOC paint to make bold, graphic, and colorful statements.

mattress free of moisture, use a double layer of wool mattress pad, a naturally fire retardant material, and then a tightly fitted sheet. Wash them at least once a week.

They say you can't machine wash and dry down because it becomes damaged. Every season I machine wash and dry my down comforters and pillows with nontoxic cleaning products. After a machine wash and dry, they are warm, fluffy and clean. I've been doing this for years and I am at a loss as to when this "damage" is going to occur. If it's at all possible, bring your pillows and blankets and wool toppers outside to air in the sun at least once a month. The sun is a natural disinfectant. If you live in a building with no place to do this, place your bedding in front of an open window in the direct sunlight.

At least every few months, or any time someone has been sick with a cold, it is a good idea to throw the pillows and duvet/blankets in the washing machine on the gentle cycle with an environmentally friendly laundry detergent.

Mattresses and Pillows

Mary Cordaro is the president and founder of Mary Cordaro Inc. *(www.marycordaro.com)*, specializing in consulting on healthy, green home building and remodeling, diagnosing and solving "sick building syndrome," and education.

Vivetique *(www.vivetique.com)* is a family-run business that offers linens, pillows, duvets, and latex mattresses for adults and children.

Bluehouse *(www.bluehouselife.com)* is an eco-friendly furnishings store that meets the following criteria: reclaimed, recycled, or recyclable products; managed resources; locally made, handmade, chemical-free, organic products; and internal company sustainability practices. They offer natural rubber and latex mattresses; chemical-free soy/hemp, rubber, buckwheat, millet, and wool pillows; organic cotton bedding, and organic cotton towels.

Hastens *(www.hastens.com)* has been making beds since 1852 from hard-wearing natural materials like horsehair, flax, wool, and pine from the forests of northern Sweden. Every bed is handmade by a master craftsman and the twenty-five year warranty slip is personally signed by that same master craftsman. The mattresses start at $12,000 and go to $60,000. Let's all hope we have clients who can afford Hastens!

Furnature *(www.furnature.com)* is a fourth-generation furniture company, dedicated to creating healthy environments. Since the early 1990s the company has been making organic bedding products. They now offer rubber

Nursery by Kati Curtis, photo by Gregory Holm

FSC wood, no-VOC paint, and nontoxic sealer make this crib safe for a little one who is teething.

mattresses for adults and children. Solid wood bed frames are made from North American Ash grown in sustainable forests. They carry organic wool and rubber pillows.

Kushtush Organics Eco Sleep Shop *(www.kushtush.com)* offers a line of organic cotton, bamboo, silk, and wool products. From a complete line of baby bedding and towels, to mattresses, pillows, duvets, bedding, and towels for adults, every product they sell is environmentally friendly and healthy. Organic pet beds are also available.

Ikea *(www.ikea.com)* sells reasonably priced mattresses that are not organic, but are PBDE free. The company follows a very long list of sustainable and environmentally friendly practices.

White Lotus *(www.whitelotus.net)* sells organic futons, sheets, duvets, and pillows.

Less is more in this rustic bedroom. The Shaker style four-post bed is made of FSC-certified wood and linens are organic cotton. Reclaimed wood floors add warmth and character to the space. A vintage painting hangs above the bed and no-VOC paint from Benjamin Moore adorns the walls.

Lifekind *(www.organicmattresses.com)* is dedicated to supporting American organic farmers and manufacturers and produces its products in the United States. The organic latex mattresses are backed by a guarantee that if you find a greener, purer mattress based on their Purity Comparison Checklist, they will give you their mattress for free. They offer crib mattresses; wool pillow tops; wool, organic cotton, rubber, and organic buckwheat hull pillows; certified organic bath towels; and organic cotton/rubber pet beds.

Pure-Rest *(www.purerest.com)* has been manufacturing healthy home and bedroom products for seventeen years. Their certified, rubber, organic mattresses start at a reasonable $800 for adults. Every product in their line has a lower-priced option for the budget conscious consumer. Their line also includes latex mattresses; rubber, wool, and organic cotton pillows; comforters; blankets; and organic cotton sheets for adults and children.

EcoBedroom *(www.ecobedroom.com)* sells latex and organic cotton futons and mattresses and can produce custom sizes, shapes, and styles. Solid maple bed frames made of sustainable wood from United States forests,

Bedroom by Lori Dennis, photo by Mark Tanner

wool mattress pads, cotton and latex pillows, organic cotton and bamboo towels, environmentally friendly pet beds, and organic pajamas are available.

BEDS AND CHILDREN'S FURNITURE

In the bedroom, use furniture that is made from FSC-certified or reclaimed solid woods attached with eco-friendly binders and finished with nontoxic materials. Fabrics, padding and cushions should be made of organic, durable, and easy-to-clean materials. This chapter will concentrate on resources for healthy bed frames and children's furniture, which is generally located in children's bedrooms. For a more complete list of furniture resources, refer to chapter 2: Furniture and Accessories.

Bed frames should be raised above the floor and

Every surface in this green showcase bedroom was covered with an eco-friendly material. The carpet, by Bentley Prince Street, is made of recycled material and is recyclable. Wall cover by Innovations is from their Environments line. Furniture is from Mitchell Gold, a longtime champion of earth-friendly manufacturing. Bedding, by Anna Sova, is made of organic cotton, as are the curtains. The throw from Livingreen is made of organic linen. And really, what could be more sustainable than a cactus?

constructed with slats that allow air to flow under mattresses and provide enough support to eliminate the need for a box spring. Bed frames should be constructed of solid wood and contain no metal.

Nontoxic finishes for cribs are mandatory because teething infants often chew on the rails to relieve pain.

Simplicity reigns in this beachside bedroom. On the walls and window molding, the architect used a soothing palate of no-VOC paint. The room takes full advantage of the natural light and connects the occupants with nature seen through generous bay of windows. Instead of air conditioning, a ceiling fan is put to work to circulate fresh air.

VivaTerra (*www.vivaterra.com*) sells beautiful platform bed frames made of reclaimed woods and finished with water-based stains and eco-friendly waxes.

Furnature (*www.furnature.com*) is a fourth-generation furniture company dedicated to creating healthy environments. Solid wood bed frames are made from North American Ash grown in sustainable forests. The slats are close enough to provide support without having to use a box spring.

EcoBedroom (*www.ecobedroom.com*) sells solid maple bed frames made of sustainable wood from United States forests.

Million Dollar Baby (*www.milliondollarbaby.com*) has an affordable collection of cribs, including a mini crib for smaller nurseries. The furniture is painted with non-toxic materials and the teething rail is phthalate safe. The cribs do not contain exposed hardware for babies to come into contact with or for incorrect installations.

Econscious Market (*www.econsciousmarket.com*), based in Boulder, Colorado, sells ecologically and socially responsible furniture for children's rooms and donates up to 10 percent of every purchase to a long list of nonprofit organizations cited on their Web site. Their online marketplace is educational in that it lists the social and environmental actions of their vendors. They encourage feedback on listed products and suggestions for things you'd like to see. I agree with them when they say the days of being in business just to make money are numbered. Giving is the new getting.

Ducduc (*www.ducducnyc.com*) closely monitors the production of its children's furniture in its Connecticut factory. All of its products use sustainably harvested wood—no MDF or particle board—and water-based and nontoxic finishes. They employ lean manufacturing systems that reduce waste and energy. The factory is a renovated and restored 1897 building on a reclaimed brownfield site. All employees are covered with health insurance and volunteer for charity work in their community. Plus the furniture is adorable.

Boom's *(www.boomusa.com)* Mini Boom collection has a clean, modern, and chic style that comes in vibrant colors. Boom's products are made from sustainably forested trees and 100 percent recycled cast aluminum, and the lacquers are all water-based. They do not associate with third world manufacturers, strictly prohibit child labor, and firmly enforce American labor laws in their Thailand factories while paying above national rates.

Iglooplay *(www.iglooplay.com)* offers sculptural furnishings that transcend generations. High-density foam covered in ultrasuede and PVC vinyl tables are easily cleaned and morph into coffee tables or junior sized loungers. All wood is obtained from sustainably yielded forestry practice. It's a very fun line that is so durable it has been approved for hospitality use.

Monte Design Group *(www.montedesign.com)* makes modern nursery furniture and has a commitment to minimizing the negative impact they make on the environment. Their foam is manufactured from natural seed-based oils like soybean. All of the foam is PDBE free. The wood they use meets the LEED requirements for no urea formaldehyde and glue used in construction is water-based and biodegradable. All products are shipped in 95 percent recycled boxes.

BEDDING AND TOWELS

When nonorganic bed linens and towels are finished and sent to you, there are still trace amounts of toxic pesticide residues on the fabrics, which you absorb through your skin while you sleep and dry yourself after bathing. Formaldehyde, classified as a human carcinogen linked to brain and lung cancer and leukemia, is the ingredient that makes most sheets stain resistant and wrinkle free. Many towels are treated with triclosan, a chemical antibacterial agent. This is overkill and it promotes super bacteria. Bamboo towels don't need any additional chemicals because bamboo has natural antibacterial properties and it can thrive without any pesticides.

Most commercial sheets and towels are made of conventional cotton, which uses a disproportional amount of pesticides and herbicides in its cultivation. The chemicals seep into the ground and bodies of water, contaminating them and harming humans,

Luxurious, organic bedding from Livingreen shares center stage with Innovations' Environments cork wall cover in this eco-friendly bedroom. Cut flowers from the garden and a succulent add just the right touch on a Mitchell Gold bedside table.

fish, and wildlife. There are entire villages in China who suffer from cancer as a result of this same type of pollution in their water supplies.

To create a healthier local and global environment, purchase organic bedding and towels. Organic fibers don't have toxic finishes and the more they are washed, the softer they become, without polluting your bedroom and the world. Bedding should always be cleaned with perfume-free and phosphate-free biodegradable detergents.

West Elm *(www.westelm.com)* offers a selection of bed linens, showers curtains, bath rugs and towels in organic cottons. The colors and patterns are current, chic, and much more than you would expect for the price. I've put these linens in multi-million-dollar homes that have won national, best design awards.

Anna Sova *(www.annasova.com)* offers some of the most luxurious organic towels, linens, and bedspreads I've ever felt. They personally inspect and approve the working conditions in every cotton co-op, silk farm, alpaca highland, and bleaching, dyeing, and sewing facility they work with and ensure fair labor conditions are being practiced. Their certified organic cotton uses no toxic

Bedroom by Lori Dennis, photo by Mark Tanner

Bedroom by Lori Dennis, photo by Ken Hayden

An FSC-certified, AFM-Safecoat-stained four poster bed creates a room within a room in this spectacular master suite designed for a hip young couple. Having triumphed over childhood cancer, the husband required a space that tread lightly on the planet and went easy on his immune system. Organic hotel linens by Lori Dennis, hand scooped bamboo floors, and organic linen curtain fabric help create a sanctuary that soothes the body and considers the environment.

fertilizers, no petrochemical pesticides, no dioxin bleaches, no heavy metal or AZO dyes, and no formaldehyde or silicon sizing. They also monogram for free.

Nandina *(www.nandina.org)* is an innovative new yarn made from organic cotton and bamboo fibers. This combination is woven into a texture that has the luster of silk and the softness of cotton while remaining extremely durable. The towels come in a wide variety of colors and patterns and are reasonably priced. The 100 percent bamboo towels are extremely soft, naturally antibacterial and antifungal, and highly absorbent.

Suite Sleep *(www.suitesleep.com)* offers reasonably priced organic cotton hotel-style linens and an organic cotton velour sheet set. They carry an infant line of mattresses, bedding, and bumpers all made in organic cotton, wool, and rubber.

Pottery Barn *(www.potterybarn.com)* has great style, there's no way around it. Their organic sheet and towel collections come in a variety of bold stripes, solids, flannels, botanicals, and hotel-style linens. They can be monogrammed for that custom touch.

Coyuchi *(www.coyuchiorganic.com)* sells beautiful heirloom-quality bedding products for adults and children made from certified organic cotton or wool. As the company became successful the founder started giving back to the farmers who grew the organic and Fair Trade certified cotton through a livestock charity. The Cow Project focuses on helping the farmers acquire livestock that contributes to the well being of their families and farms. The manure and urine from these cows are collected for organic fertilizer and pesticides, and milk provides additional nutrition for the villagers. The cows are respected, well treated and loved by their owners.

Indika *(www.indikahome.com)* offers organic hand-loomed towels, sheets, and duvets. Also available are duvets and shams made of hemp/silk combinations. They will customize linen orders.

BambroTex *(www.bambrotex.com)* is a wholesaler of bamboo towels available in any color.

Amenity Home *(www.amenity-home.com)* carries a stylish collection of nature-inspired, large-scaled graphic prints in certified organic cotton, hemp, alpaca, and linen. All goods are manufactured in the United States by conscientious manufacturers who use eco-friendly dyes and natural fibers. The nursery collection consists of bold, delightful storybook scenes of animals and nature. All fabrics and dyes are organic. These ladies make fun, relaxing prints with a warm, modern aesthetic.

Rawganique *(www.rawganique.com)* sells sweatshop-free, certified organic hemp and linen products made in the United States, Europe, and Canada. The company carries the world's first and only organically grown hemp towels, pure and sustainable as they come. They offer fine French linen sheets made without chemical finishes, heavy dyes, or toxic finishes at half the cost of competitors.

Loop *(www.looporganic.com)* sells sweatshop-free certified organic towels, sheets, and blankets processed with no harsh chemicals and finished for softness and purity. Bed linens come in a rich palette of earth colors and a funky leaf pattern. The towel collection offers a line of current colors in a fluffy, super soft, long-looped terry.

SHOWER CURTAINS

Instead of cheap PVC curtains which offgas toxins and need frequent replacement, buy hemp shower curtains. For under a hundred dollars, you will get a curtain that will last a lifetime. Hemp, used for ship's sails, is water resistant and extremely durable. Most of them are pretty

Letting a child's imagination run wild doesn't mean sacrificing safety or heath. In this fire engine station of a bedroom, recycled tire flooring cushions daring jumps from the top of the engine, and low-VOC paint reduces toxic fumes. (At the time we designed this room, darker colors were not readily available in no-VOC paints. Today you have a much, much wider variety of available and affordable no-VOC colors.) Anna Sova organic linens ensure a restful night.

Bedroom by Lori Dennis, photo by Christian Romero

plain; they look like unfinished painting canvases. I took matters into my own hands and wrote cute phrases in French all over mine, like "time to shave your legs" and "no kitties allowed." Anyone who can read French gets a real kick out of the curtain. Those who can't just think it looks cool. If you want to go the custom route, buy organic outdoor fabric and have them sewn into a panel curtain.

Rawganique *(www.rawganique.com)* sells sweatshop-free, VOC-free curtains that come in three sizes and have been recommended by Natural Home, Elle and USA Today.

Gaiam *(www.gaiam.com)* sells a chemical-free linen shower curtain with rust proof grommets.

Satara, Inc.'s *(www.satara-inc.com)* cotton curtain is grown without pesticides and processed without toxic chemicals or chlorine bleach. Their hemp curtain absorbs and channels water efficiently and comes in tub size.

West Elm *(www.westelm.com)* is another great option. Organic cotton, bold color curtains never looked so good for the price. They also offer a vinyl-free liner.

childhood bumps are a rite of passage which teach humans how to balance and avoid falling. Poisonous chemical carpeting is the furthest thing from providing a safe environment for your child to grow. Particularly troublesome are wall-to-wall carpets that can never be removed or cleaned properly. As these carpets get older they have unavoidable dust mites and microbes proliferating in them. Alternative materials like bamboo, wool, organic cotton, vintage rags, nontoxic rubber mats, and eco-friendly, replaceable floor tiles are much, much better solutions for removable rugs in bedrooms.

This chapter will focus on rugs for children's rooms. Please refer to chapter 2: Furniture and Accessories for additional rug sources.

Floor Score *(www.floorscore.com)* sells about ten different styles of rubber flooring tiles. They are made from recycled tires, come in a wide selection of colors, and are all easy to install.

Green Earth Market *(www.greenearthmarket.com)* sells organic cotton rag rugs, made with scrap organic fabric from our sheets and upholstery items. They are hand woven by an Amish widow, come in custom colors, and are machine washable.

With twice the stregth of cotton, Gaiam's *(www.gaiam.com)* hemp rugs are naturally mildew resistant and softer than sisal or jute. The elegant look of a woven hemp rug fits into any style décor. Also check out their naturally antifungal, antislip, cork bath mat.

VivaTerra *(www.vivaterra.com)* sells naturally antibacterial bamboo rugs in three earthy colors and multiple sizes.

Flokati *(www.flokati.com)* has a large collection of natural wool rugs in many colors, sizes, and patterns. They're great for kids' rooms because they can be thrown in a commercial washing machine or shaken outdoors and left in the sunlight to disinfect.

WINDOW TREATMENTS

Reseach indicates that a bedroom should be pitch-black, as light pollution cuts down on the production of melatonin. Wood and bamboo blinds work well in bedrooms because they block light and are easily cleaned. Fabric window coverings have the advantage of keeping the room warmer in winter months and potentially pitch-black when blackout liners are added—but they are more difficult to clean. When selecting fabric treatments, avoid materials treated with harmful chemical finishes. (These are usually added to make curtains hang straight without wrinkles.) Instead select washable curtains made from organic fibers which are easy to remove and replace.

(See chapter 3: Fabrics for window treatment sources.)

Vibrant, fun, affordable, and machine washable drapery panels help to prevent allergies from dust buildup and separate space, providing privacy in this young boy's bedroom.

AREA RUGS

Wood floors, covered with area rugs, are the best for the bedrooms. Wood floors are softer than stone or tile and area rugs help to accomplish that cozy feeling which is so desirable in a bedroom. It is especially important to frequently clean area rugs in bedrooms and nurseries, more so than other rooms of the house. Because you spend the most time in these rooms, more accumulation of dead human and pet cells, hair, dust, and dander settles in these spaces. Without frequently cleaning, you are basically providing a free buffet for bacteria and dust mites.

Avoid using new wall-to-wall carpet or synthetic area rugs in children's rooms. A child who plays on a synthetic rug is extremely susceptible to the harmful chemicals that offgas into the room. Parents are afraid their toddlers will get hurt on wood floors, but a few

9 GREEN BUILDING

Over the last few years, the eco-friendly buzz was mostly about driving hybrid and electric cars, but there is a much bigger problem we should have been addressing: man-made buildings. Homes and offices account for about half of the energy use and greenhouse gas emissions worldwide. This is a staggering number when compared to cars' and light trucks' percentage, which is only 9 percent. The traditional methods used to build and operate our homes contribute to smog, acid rain, and global warming. Thankfully, there is now a growing interest in building and certifying structures that are less harmful to our environment and the people occupying these spaces. Rating systems like Build It Green, Energy Star, and LEED are becoming more popular as people begin to realize the economic, environmental, and health benefits of building green structures. The less energy and raw materials that are used and the more efficient these buildings become, the less pollution they will generate.

WHAT IS A GREEN HOME?

A green home is one that uses less resources, energy, and water than a conventional home. It has better indoor air quality and is healthier for the people living in it. Green homes are also more durable and cost less money to operate. The National Homebuilders Association expects that in 2010 over 10 percent of new homes built will be green. This is great news when you consider that over the last twenty years the average square footage of a house went from about 1,500 to nearly 2,500 square feet. With about a million new homes being built in the United States every year, an enormous amount of raw materials and energy is used and millions of tons of waste are created. Most of these homes are not built efficiently so the energy it takes to heat, cool, light, and power them is even more astounding.

For ecological and economic reasons people are downsizing and building green. Many states, municipalities, and utilities offer incentives, tax breaks, and rebates to do this. Fortunately this is resulting in more people in the building industry looking for products that contain recycled content, have a positive impact on indoor air quality, save energy and water, and are produced locally to reduce the environmental costs of transportation. A reasonable concern for anyone building a home is: will it cost more to go green? The answer is not necessarily. New technologies have opened the doors to more efficient and less wasteful building, and alternative energy has become less expensive and more accessible.

This chapter will help you locate various products and services that will help you and your building team find suitable resources for your green building venture.

SIZE AND STYLE

Make sure the square footage is not bigger than needed to avoid wasting materials, labor, and energy. Build only as big as you truly need. It's a simple fact: the bigger the structure, the more you impact the environment. While it is important to build smaller, it is equally important to build smart. Good design is green design. The ASID Regreen Program puts it best: you can have a quality project that is not green, but you cannot have a green project that is also not a quality project. You cannot specify materials just because they are efficient without considering how they work in the space effectively. You would be wasting your efforts if you just make a list of green products and start dropping them into your plans without really considering how they will aesthetically affect the project. If a building is not beautiful and functional, you haven't done your job and, worse, you risk it having to be remodeled shortly after you're gone. This is a good way to ruin your reputation and waste money, time, and resources. And wasting anything in this process is the polar opposite of what we are trying to accomplish.

SITE

Green building from the ground up or remodeling existing structures will require the efforts of an entire team of building professionals. Careful planning from the beginning stages can help to reduce some of your carbon footprint in this process. Begin with site location (for new construction). Choose a site that is close to public transportation or services you will use daily. Contrary to popular belief, selecting a site in an urban area, one where you can walk or ride your bike to public transportation, work, shopping, recreation, and entertainment is green.

Locate or redesign the building and surrounding landscaping so that it takes advantage of what the climate has to offer.

If you have the opportunity to reuse a building, take it. Especially in a run-down, urban center, adaptively rehabilitating historic buildings is one of the most sustainable actions you can take. Many cities have urban revitalization programs and offer incentives to update these buildings. When you add green to your agenda, you can bet your project is slated for a home run.

After the project site is known, the next consideration

is deconstruction. Notice I did not say demolition. The difference is using an informed labor force to assist in preserving all the materials they can. Bricks, lumber, salvaged architectural materials, doors, knobs, sinks, and almost every material you can think of can be diverted from landfills and recycled or reused in your project. Dispose of waste from construction using an eco-friendly approach instead of using landfills as your "go to" option. Landfills are bloated with waste and the incineration of construction waste creates air pollution. Both of these methods disregard the value of lost resources. Work with your team to think of every way you can minimize construction waste. Be resourceful by doing things like moving the old kitchen cabinets to the garage for storage. Sorting for salvage, recycle, and donation should become routine on a green construction site. You can contact your municipal recycling facility for the best options in your area. The goal is to keep as much out of the trash as possible.

If the soil is being displaced during construction, limit vegetation from being removed to help prevent soil erosion. Collect any soil that is removed during construction and reuse it in areas that will be landscaped. When they built the Getty Center in Los Angeles, one of the conditions was that all of the dirt that was dug out for foundation had to be reused on the site. If they managed to rearrange tens of thousands of pounds of dirt, you can do it on your site too.

If you're going for LEED Certification, site selection and demolition waste are two prerequisites. You will have to start thinking green at the very beginning.

Inhabitat is a great architectural Web site. In their blog they offer a series of information on different topics called Green Building 101. The following link also gives five measures you can take to create a more sustainable site: *www.inhabitat.com/2006/07/05/green-building-101-sustainable-sites/*

BUILDING DESIGN

Good green building design has an abundance of natural light and airflow. The success of these two elements largely depends on the design of your window, heating, and cooling systems.

Natural and Artificial Light

If you have the opportunity to decide where windows and doors will be, think about what rooms are being used during different times of the day. Provide opportunities for plenty of natural daylight. Make sure that the natural light source coincides with the way the rooms are used and allow for cross ventilation. Natural light and a lot of windows are great ways to reduce ambient lighting in the day, but poorly designed placement of these windows can lead to overheating and excessive energy use for cooling. Make wise placement decisions like not placing the largest windows on the west side. They will receive sun during the hottest parts of the day making cooling the space less efficient. Clerestory windows on the west side are a good option for extremely hot climates where you want natural light in the afternoon to evening.

Provide an appropriate mix of ambient and task lighting. During the daylight hours, if possible, make sure all ambient lighting is provided by natural daylight. When daylight is unavailable, try solar tubes. Solar tubes and skylights reduce dependence on artificial light sources on sunny days and are a good way to get natural light into rooms with no windows, like hallways and laundry rooms. If the solar tubes are equipped with fluorescent fixtures, they will function as lights in the evening.

For nighttime, use the most energy efficient lighting possible. Indirect fluorescent lighting is effective and has come a long way in its color quality. For task lighting, good choices are direct sources from compact fluorescents and LED light fixtures.

Solatube (*www.solatube.com*) is the world's leading manufacturer of tubular skylights, offering the highest performance products in the industry.

Solar Track (*www.solar-track.com*) offers both skylights and solar tubes, which track the sun (for maximum exposure in mornings and evenings) and are photovoltaic powered.

Operable windows are an essential component of natural airflow and light. The key is to make sure the windows you choose are energy efficient. There is no blanket remedy for choosing the right window. There are four Energy Star climate zones in North America: Northern Climate (Minneapolis, MN) which requires mostly heating; the North/Central (Washington, DC) and South/Central (Phoenix, AZ), which require heating and cooling; and the Southern Climate (Miami, FL) which requires mostly cooling. Depending on where the project is, you will have different needs. The Efficient Windows Collaborative (EWC) is a member organization with a great Web site to help you with your choices. The site provides unbiased information on the benefits of energy efficient windows, descriptions of how they work, and recommendations for selection and use. I especially like this site because it is so easy to use and has a thorough list of eco-friendly vendors for windows and skylights. Another bonus is that it provides detailed information on how to get monetary compensation for homeowners who install energy-efficient windows. Any time you can show a client how to save money, you help enforce why design professionals are necessary. (*www.efficientwindows.org*)

There are many technical facts about selecting windows

with good energy performance. You can begin by looking at the Energy Star ratings. Some of the other universal elements of efficient windows are: multi-glazing layers (triple is the best), low-conductivity gas fills, seals on insulated units, heat-reflective (low-emissivity) coatings, multiple low-e coatings, advanced weather stripping, and new frame systems. Exterior shading can also play a role. It is best to work with a trusted local window professional for site-specific fenestration decisions.

There is a debate about whether plastic or wood windows are better for the environment. Most people think that wood is a better choice for the environment, but that may not be the case. Vinyl windows can be made of sustainable, environmentally friendly, low-maintenance materials that last for decades and do not emit toxins. Wood windows tend to be less efficient and require more maintenance and faster replacements than plastic. Plastic windows come in both ABS and vinyl (PVC). ABS is a better choice. Windows made of ABS do not contain chlorine so there is no risk of dioxin generation during an accidental fire or incineration at the end of the product's life.

When installing windows in wet areas like bathrooms, showers, or tubs, select a window that has a moisture tolerant frame made of plastic or fiberglass. Metal or wood frames will break down when they come in contact with water on a daily basis. Sills must also be made of a surface that is impermeable to water and constructed as if it was on the exterior. Solid material sills are better than tiled surfaces. If you are going to use a tiled surface, however, use an epoxy grout.

Gorell Windows & Doors (*www.gorell.com*) has again been recognized by the U.S. Department of Energy and the U.S. Environmental Protection Agency as the winner of the prestigious Energy Star Partner of the Year Award for the sixth straight year. Gorell received the Sustained Excellence Award, bestowed only on organizations that have won the Energy Star Partner of the Year award three or more consecutive times, for the fourth consecutive year. Based on these awards and the company's practices, I would feel comfortable calling their windows green.

Loewen (*www.loewen.com*) is a company that sells all over North America in stores like Home Depot and Lowe's. Their Heat Smart window line is exceeding sturdy, energy-efficient, and tested to withstand arctic temperatures as well as searing tropical heat.

Paramount (*www.paramountwindows.com*) has been a leader in energy-efficient windows for almost six decades. They offer wood, metal, and plastic windows with a series of high-performance glass systems emphasizing reflective glass and insulated spacers.

Blur the line of indoor and outdoor completely with Nana Wall System (*www.nanawall.com*). The new system is Energy Star rated with heat mirror glazing which is as good of an insulator as a solid wall only it allows tons of natural light to come into a space and open completely to the outside when the weather allows.

Natural and Artificial Ventilation, Heating, and Cooling

Use materials and methods that aid in the natural heating and cooling of the structure. "Build tight, ventilate right" is a common saying in green building. A tightly sealed home improves comfort and indoor air quality—as long as you have specified nontoxic surface materials and furnishings. When you seal holes and cracks in the home's envelope and in heating and cooling duct systems you can reduce drafts, moisture, dust, pollen, and noise. In addition to using less energy because they don't have to work as hard, energy-efficient heating and air systems improve the overall atmosphere of a home. We know that proper window placement and type can help to lessen the load on heating and cooling systems.

Ceiling Fans

Combine good design with ceiling fans to avoid using air conditioning. If your climate is unforgiving and you do use air conditioning, choose Energy Star rated systems. They will reduce energy consumption by 20–40 percent over conventional units. Make sure to install programmable thermostats for both heating and cooling systems.

G Squared Art (*www.g2art.com*), a 1% for the Planet member, offers a unique ceiling fan line.

The Modern Fan Co. (*www.modernfan.com*) has an impressive selection of ceiling fans and they offer color-corrected compact fluorescent compatible fixtures.

Exhaust Fans

Exhaust fans are an important component in a tightly sealed building. Use them while cooking in the kitchen and showering/bathing in bathrooms if there are no windows. It is good green practice to design bathrooms with operable windows or good sources of ventilation to prevent mold growth.

For bathrooms with no windows, make sure to install a quiet and energy-efficient fan. My favorites are from Panasonic. They're quiet, efficient and reliable, and they look good. Kitchen ventilation is equally as important as you may recall from the appliances chapter. (*www.panasonic.com*)

Radiant Heating

For heating a home, radiant heat has a number of advantages over forced air. It is more efficient than baseboard and forced air because no energy is lost when the heat

Since heat rises, radiant heating is one of the most efficient methods to warm a space. Radiant systems can be installed inside or on exterior patios. Walking barefoot on a warm floor, especially on a cold day, is a luxury we should all experience.

Photo by Joseph Treves

rises. The lack of forced air is advantageous to people with allergies. Water-based systems (hydronic) use little electricity. With radiant heat, unlike central air, you can zone different areas of the home for different temperatures. Radiant heating systems can be installed under most flooring: wood, concrete, stone, and tile. And there is more freedom in the interior design because you do not have to consider the placement of vents. If you're working on a tight budget (and who isn't?) and you can't afford radiant heating throughout the interior, consider at least putting it in the bathrooms.

Hannel Radiant Direct (*www.radiantdirect.com*) is a company that designs and manufactures high-quality, easy-to-install, and affordable hydronic radiant heat flooring.

Warm Your Floor (*www.warmyourfloor.com*) offers a variety of electric, radiant floor heating. For snowy climates they also have snow and ice melting cables for exterior walks and driveways.

If you have forced air for cooling and heating, consider mechanical, whole-house filtration systems or, at the very least, filters on your heating intakes, the furnace itself, and vents to each room. Some air quality specialists recommend a "bake off" after new construction or a remodel to speed up the offgassing of chemicals in the residence. Plan to vacate the house for a few days, turn the temperature and airflow up higher than usual, open all the windows and continue for at least three days. This is said to help release the toxic chemicals faster and make the air cleaner to breathe when you finally occupy the space.

Finally, make sure the garage is sealed off from the rest of the house. Toxic fumes from cars are the last thing you want seeping into your home.

MATERIALS

The best advice I can give on choosing materials is to try to select products that come from renewable sources and don't contribute to toxins that pollute our planet.

Drywall

At a million square feet produced every year, drywall is the most common indoor building material in the United States. It is problematic due to its intense energy usage (1 percent of the United States' annual energy consumption) and raw material use during production. Specifying sustainable alternatives to traditional drywall will help to eliminate millions of tons of harmful carbon emissions into our environment.

Greentech Wallboard (*www.spertech.com*) is a viable substitute for drywall. With 98 percent recycled content, it is naturally mildew-resistant, fire-retardant, cost-competitive, and performs like conventional drywall.

Eco Rock by Serious (*www.seriousmaterials.com*) uses 80 percent recycled materials in their mold resistant and low emitting drywall product. Eighty percent less energy is used to produce Eco Rock, and it is designed to be fully reutilized as a pH additive for soil or a raw material for new Eco Rock.

Reclaimed Wood

In the United States, most reclaimed wood comes from old buildings, barns, factories, and warehouses. The reclaimed wood comes from old-growth timber that was harvested from trees that were bigger and older than anything that is harvested today. This results in wood that possesses superior characteristics to new growth lumber.

Headquartered in Portland, Oregon, AltruWood (*www.altruwood.com*) specializes in reclaimed lumber and FSC-certified wood products harvested from responsible sources. They are also FSC-certified and specialize in locating materials that are difficult to source like FSC-certified western red cedar and Ipe decking. They are dedicated to being the most reliable supplier of green building products in North America.

FSC-Certified Wood Products

FSC-certified wood has been harvested from forests that practice environmentally and economically responsible forestry. The certified wood products are verified by a third party as originating from well-managed forests. Green Spec regards the FSC standards as the most rigorous and the only certification system with a well-established chain of custody certification.

Allard Lumber (*www.allardlumber.com*) offers FSC products which meet or exceed state and federal regulations for environmental protection. They manage woodlots by determining your needs and take ecological requirements into consideration before they begin logging (cutting) your order.

Cascadia (*www.cascadiaforestgoods.com*) is one of those companies that not only pays attention to the environment, but also gives back to people with social and economic programs. They work to eliminate illegal logging and improve the management of valuable and threatened forests. Specializing in timbers and solid wood flooring, paneling, siding, and decking, their wood comes from reclaimed sources or from places where sustainable forestry is practiced. They can customize orders for odd sizes or patterns.

Engineered Wood

While it is not free from ecological concerns, engineered products can provide a significant advantage over solid wood by utilizing fast-growing, small diameter trees. If you choose to use engineered wood, be sure that you are not selecting products with formaldehyde or phenol-formaldehyde binders.

Standard Structures (*www.standardstructures.com*) is a manufacturer of custom-engineered roof and flooring systems for the residential and commercial construction markets. Nearly all of their products can be manufactured with FSC certification. In addition, all of their products are engineered with low-VOC, exterior grade adhesives which contain no added urea-formaldehyde.

Innovative Wood Concepts makes framing studs out of wood scraps recycled from construction sites and truss companies by finger-jointing them using water-based glue. Waste from production is turned into mulch and animal bedding. According to the company, they kept over 3.5 million linear feet of wood from reaching the landfill last year. Their phone number is (435)674-4555 (they don't have a Web site).

Cement

Cement production is energy intensive and polluting. Using concrete mixes containing recycled content, like fly ash, is more desirable. Up to 60 percent of the conventional portland cement can be substituted with fly ash, which is a waste product of coal-fired plants. It actually makes the concrete stronger and easier to work with compared to unadulterated portland cement mix. Other industrial waste products like ground blast furnace slag and rice hull ash can be added to portland cement making the process less energy intensive and keeping the waste out of landfills.

Boral Material Technologies (*www.boralmti.com*) is a leading marketer of fly ash and all coal combustion products. With more than four decades of experience marketing fly ash to the concrete industry, Boral is a pioneer in the development of new construction material technologies.

Holcim's Envirocore and GranChem cements (*www.holcim.com*) are made from recyclable materials that are mixed with portland cement. The result is a good looking and durable product. The factory uses alternative sourcing fuels, decreased emission practices, and efficient transportation choices. They've set a goal of reducing the CO_2 intensity of their production by 20 percent in 2010.

When concrete is used as a finish surface, coloring pigments are sometimes desired to produce architectural interest. The great thing about using cement as a finish material is that there is no need for additional coatings. Most sealants and finishers on the market are toxic and produce negative environmental impacts.

Hoover Color Corporation (*www.hoovercolor.com*) offers EnvironOxide pigments. Iron-rich sludge from abandoned mine-shafts is transformed into a trio of pigments that are brown in color, yet have a range of undertones from red to yellow to blue. The use of these pigments can contribute toward LEED accreditation.

Doors

Reclaimed doors and composite material doors are the most eco-friendly selections for interior doors. Reclaimed doors obviously make the least environmental impact and remove the need for disposal. Composite doors are beneficial because they use recycled content and fewer raw materials in their construction. If you want new material, solid wood doors, be sure to specify FSC-certified wood doors. No matter which door type you prefer, the use of glass panes in doors is an effective way to illuminate rooms with little or no light.

Liberty Valley Doors (*www.libertyvalleydoors.com*) has an FSC-certified line of rediscovered wood doors made from 100 percent reclaimed wood. The factory is solar powered and has a long list of eco-friendly behaviors including an employee e-waste program.

Humabuilt (*www.humabuilt.com*) sells an attractive, affordable interior door made of renewable resources and recycled content. The wheat core doors are free of formaldehyde and can be stained or painted. I actually like them unfinished. What also impressed me about the company is that it is one of the few manufacturers who understand Bau-Biologie.

INSULATION

Insulation reduces cracks and gaps that allow unwanted moisture and air to enter. A well-insulated structure is the key to conserving resources and saving energy. When you begin with a well-insulated building with proper ventilation, you have an essential starting point to a more comfortable and efficient structure. Good insulation also reduces noise pollution and allows for private, peaceful enjoyment of a residence.

Blanket or batt insulations, especially fiberglass products, are typically inexpensive but require meticulous installation to minimize air leaks around openings that can compromise the wall's overall performance. Using a nontoxic insulation spray doesn't require the precision of batt insulation but may be a more expensive application. When selecting an insulation product consider one that has high recycled content, renewable materials, little or no indoor air quality concerns, and superior performance for air tightness and management of moisture. Also, be sure to pay special attention to roofs and attics.

Wool Batt and Spray Insulation

Wool is an environmentally friendly renewable resource. It is naturally flame retardant. Some say it is a better thermal insulator than other fibers because of its ability to absorb and release moisture from the air. When temperatures rise outside, the wool is heated and it releases moisture, which has a cooling effect on the fiber and the building. When outside temperatures decrease the wool absorbs moisture, which causes a heating effect. It is a superior sound block. Wool is noncarcinogenic and doesn't cause irritation to the installer or the homeowner. (It can be installed without wearing gloves.) In addition to being recyclable and a pest repellant, wool is a very efficient absorber of indoor pollutants. Research has shown that wool can permanently absorb and retain high levels of formaldehyde, nitrogen, and sulphur dioxide. Go wool.

Good Shepard Wool (*www.goodshepardwool.com*) is a provider of wool insulation. They also have a wool rope product that can insulate log cabins.

Applegate Insulation (*www.applegateinsulation.com*) is environmentally friendly and made of 80 to 85 percent recycled newsprint. The manufacturing process of the cellulose insulation uses one-fifth the energy of fiberglass and generates virtually zero emissions.

Bonded Logic's product line (*www.bondedlogic.com*) includes both spray and batting natural fiber insulation products that range in thickness and density for thermal- and acoustic-specific needs. Their products are easy to install and healthy, made from recycled content materials without harmful chemicals or VOC concerns.

RENEWABLE ENERGY

With unlimited potential, solar, wind, and geothermal energies are clean, efficient, and sustainable forms of renewable energy. Once a system is installed, the supply of energy is free and can even be sold back to the utility

Spray in insulation being applied in a new construction project.

Photo by Joseph Treves

companies when there is an excess supply. A concern with using wind or solar power is variability of the source. The combination of wind and solar hybrid systems helps to ensure your energy source will remain constant.

Humans have used wind to grind corn, pump water, or drive ships for well over a thousand years. In the end of the 19th century we began using wind energy to produce electricity. When oil and coal were so inexpensive over the last hundred years, wind technology was pushed to the side. Today wind power has made a comeback as a viable energy source. If you've ever traveled the 10 Freeway from Los Angeles to Palm Springs, you will see one of the biggest wind farms in the United States. Massive windmills turn in the desert wind providing alternative and clean energy to power plants in the area. I drive by about twice a year and there always seem to be more windmills turning. It's a sign of the times and a reminder that we are headed to a more sustainable future when it comes to energy.

Bergey Windpower (*www.bergey.com*) is a leading supplier of small wind turbines. The company has been in business for thirty years and has a network of dealers around the world. Their turbines allow homeowners to produce clean energy in urban, suburban, and remote locations. They also carry systems that help to boost the performance of solar electric systems.

Southwest Windpower (*www.windenergy.com*) is the world's leading producer of small wind turbines for on- and off-grid homes. They offer a wide range of wind power systems.

Geothermal

For several decades, geothermal energy has been used to heat and air condition buildings. Essentially, a geothermal heat pump taps the earth's surface energy to power heating and cooling systems for the home. The result is a green energy

Using the sun as an energy source is one of the most obvious ways to power a building without harming the environment. Fortunately the price of materials and installation continues to drop as more residential and commercial structures opt for solar power. I remember seeing panels go up all over the place when I was a kid and wondered what happened when it seemed to completely stop in the '80s. I'm so glad to see folks hoisting panels up on their roofs again

pump that saves energy and doesn't harm the environment.

With a wide range of residential geothermal products and a well-trained network of dealers and installers, Water Furnace (*www.waterfurnace.com*) is a leader in the industry.

Whisper Energy (*www.whisperenergy.com*) offers various green energy systems including geothermal and wind power with a strong company-wide commitment to innovating new products for a cleaner environment.

Solar Panels

Solar panels, also known as photovoltaic systems, use sunlight to produce electricity. Small systems can be used to heat hot water tanks, garden pathways, and backup power needs. The larger stand-alone systems, which can run an entire home's electricity needs without being hooked up to the grid, require storage battery banks so energy is still available when the sun isn't shining. When you hear about selling electricity back to the utilities, this is referring to a system that is hooked up to the grid and metered.

Suntech (*www.suntech-power.com*) is one of the largest solar module producers in the world. As a publicly traded company, their R&D department has the financial advantage to continuously develop new, more efficient and architecturally innovative solar energy products for

lower prices. In addition, you can learn about the very interesting history of solar energy in the United States on their Web site.

Most people have seen solar panels on the roofs of buildings, and while they're highly functional, they are not the most attractive architectural features. Now photovoltaic panels can also be architecturally incorporated into the roofs and windows. Schott Solar (*www.schottsolar.com*) offers both systems and they are gorgeous.

WATER CONSERVATION

Even though the Earth is comprised mostly of water, a great deal of it is non-potable, salt water. Much of the fresh water is locked in the polar ice caps and unavailable to humans for consumption. The reality is that approximately 1 percent of the water on our planet is currently available for us to drink. UNESCO has predicted that by 2020 water shortage will be a serious worldwide problem. We are already seeing many rivers, like the Colorado, being drained at a rate that doesn't allow them to ever reach the ocean. Water conservation is the top green priority. Much of the fresh water used in the home is flushed down the toilet and wasted while running the water, waiting for it to get hot. Designing water-wise systems that reuse greywater for landscaping and flushing toilets is a no-brainer, as is installing localized water heaters that make the water hot immediately. Storing rainwater in tanks and using filters to clean it also makes a lot of sense. Practicing water conservation will help to ensure that future generations have clean water to drink.

Plumbing Systems

Install low-flow plumbing (see appliances chapter for fixtures). Since they function as well and cost the same as conventional features, this will be one of the easier water conservation acts that you can practice.

Greywater systems require more planning and money, but result in saving the 30 to 35 percent of fresh water that is literally flushed down the toilet each and every day. The greywater systems recycle, clean, and reuse the water from sinks (not including the kitchen), showers, baths, and laundry machines. Greywater systems are equally beneficial for irrigating landscape. Check your local state regulations, as some will not allow you to irrigate with greywater.

Brac Systems (*www.bracsystems.com*) carries residential greywater recycling systems to be used to filter water from laundry and dishwashing machines, sinks and showers.

SoCal Contractor (*www.socalcontractor.com*) is a green building company that educates and installs greywater systems for residential and commercial buildings.

Photos by Joseph Treves

I like to call this photo "water conservation central." It includes a whole house water filtration system, on demand water heaters (which are, of course, powered by the sun), a greywater system and an electronic brain to regulate useage according to climate conditions.

Clivus Multrum (*www.clivusmultrum.com*) designs and installs greywater systems throughout North America. Each system is custom designed for unique site conditions.

A very cool video about greywater systems: *http://www.dwell.com/videos/the-bathroom-reinvented-hyphae.html*

Water Heaters

There is a debate about whether tankless or conventional water heaters are more eco-friendly. With a tankless water heater, the water comes out hot immediately so you don't need to keep it running while you wait for hot water, but tankless, electric, instant demand systems use a high amount of energy to operate. (Gas-powered models are a better option.) Water heater tanks can be kept insulated to help reduce energy to heat them and they require less energy to heat the water than tankless models. Tank water heaters can also be heated by solar power. In Israel, almost every house uses the solar powered tank water heater system. I tested their system and thought it worked pretty well.

Built in the United States, Phoenix Solar Water Heaters (*www.phoenixsolarwaterheaters.info*) have solar-powered, combination space and water heaters with a 90 percent efficiency rating. On cloudy days you have a back up natural gas or propane system to ensure hot water.

Bosch (*www.boschhotwater.com*) is a leader in common sense hot water technology. Some of the products in the line are Energy Star rated; all are super-efficient.

The Geospring Water Heater (*www.geappliances.com/heatpump-hot-water-heater*) has an electric heat pump to move hot water quickly to the source. This innovative product can reduce water heating operating costs up to 62 percent per year and save thousands of gallons of water that is wasted running while you wait for it to get hot.

Rainwater Harvesting

Most commonly coming from roofs, the collection of rainwater provides homeowners with soft water for irrigation and potable uses.

Rain Tank Depot (*www.raintankdepot.com*) carries several brands of above-ground and underground rainwater collection tanks. I particularly like Aquadra Systems, which offers an above-ground seventy-five gallon tank made of 20 percent post-consumer recycled plastic. They come in seven vivid colors.

Finally, consider installing a water filter system for not only drinking water, but bathing water. Carbon filters remove chlorine and pesticides from your water supply.

The solar powered water distillation systems by SolAqua (*www.solacqua.com*) remove impurities such as salts and heavy metals.

Rain Tank Depot (*www.raintankdepot.com*) has several systems that offer UV, solar, electric, or reverse osmosis technology for water purification.

LANDSCAPE

Outdoor living is our daily connection with nature. There are steps we can take in exterior design to improve the sustainability of a project. We can positively manipulate the landscape to prevent storm water runoff and retain soil by constructing permeable surfaces and green roofs. Energy use to heat and cool the structure can be greatly reduced by proper planting, shading, and the inclusion of solar exterior lights. Toxins and waste can be prevented by selection of proper surface materials. Taking the extra step to think about the way the exterior looks and functions will help your make your endeavor, from the inside to out, a truly green one.

Shade

Controlling the amount of sun that enters windows or lands on walls can significantly reduce cooling energy loads. Think shade, shade, shade—from trees, canopies, and pergolas. Your home, driveway, sidewalk, and paved terraces all absorb heat throughout the day, storing it like a battery and then radiating it back into the atmosphere at night. When possible, keep these areas shaded. Awnings, plantings, or arbors on the property help to minimize the effects of the sun's rays. Although interior shading systems can help to regulate the interior temperature, exterior shading systems are more effective. In cold climates many large southwest windows are a good idea when overhangs are used and deciduous trees are planted in front of them. In winter, when the leaves are gone, it allows sun to warm the building, reducing cooling loads. In the summer, when the sun is high in the sky, large overhangs keep the windows in the shade. Trees provide additional climate control against wind. Evergreen trees and shrubs, planted on the north or west side of the home will act as wind breaks. The type of plantings will depend on your climate. Consult with a local nursery about indigenous plants for your region.

Photo by Joseph Treves

Laying sheets that prevent weeds from sprouting eliminates the need to use toxic herbicides in landscape management. Tiny spaces in the material allow water to drain into the ground instead of running off into the storm drains. This helps to alleviate overburdened municipal water treatment plants and keeps toxins out of lakes and oceans. Spot-focused, drip irrigation efficiently waters only the intended plant, not the sidewalk or your car, conserving precious H_2O.

Water Runoff and Heat Island Effect

Especially in urban areas where there is a large amount of impervious surfaces, heat radiates back into the environment adding to global warming. It not only increases air conditioning loads, it generates more smog. Using highly reflective pavement and roofs or green roofs can help to minimize the heat island effect.

The runoff from roofs, sidewalks, driveways, and other impervious surfaces leads to soil erosion and pollution of waterways. Chemicals, like oil, pesticides, and fertilizers, that build up on impervious surfaces can be broken down if they are allowed to drain into the earth and filter naturally. This occurs when you maximize the amount of permeable ground and roof surface with porous materials and use landscape features where water can collect and infiltrate. For pathways, walkways, driveways, and parking spots consider permeable pavement soil retention product, gravel, or decomposed granite.

Invisible Structures (*www.invisiblestructures.com*) specializes in 100 percent recycled content, soil erosion control mats. The plastic structure is installed underground and can be used for parking spots, walkways, slopes, or landscaping. They mitigate storm water runoff, filter pollutants, reduce urban heat island effect, and reduce soil erosion.

Green Roofs

Perhaps one of my favorite sustainable building systems is a green roof. In addition to the environmental benefits, I love the idea of using every square inch of a building. Already common in Europe and Canada, green roof systems, for low-slope roofs, protect the roof membrane, reduce storm water flows, and help green the built environment through rooftop plantings. Green roofs can detain over half of the rainwater from a typical storm. A green roof includes drainage, geotextile, soil, and vegetation layers. Multilayered green roof systems are thicker than conventional roofs, so additional structural support is typically required. (I've been on more than one project where the owners wanted to build a green roof, but were deterred when they found out the existing structure wouldn't support the weight of a green roof. Make sure to alert them to this during the planning phase.) A thick sod of native grasses interspersed with wildflowers can be a wonderful architectural element that also helps to reduce heat gain. Native plants and proper soils, however, are usually more appropriate and are probably less expensive. An added bonus is that plantings also absorb CO_2. If a green roof is not in the cards for you on a project, paint or cover the roof in a light color to reduce heat island effect.

Although Emory Knoll Farms (*www.greenroof-plants.com*) specializes in Maryland, Pennsylvania, Washington D.C., Virginia, North Carolina, and Ohio, it's a fifth-generation farm that deals exclusively with plants for green roofs. I'd give them a quick call or check out their Web site before I went to my local nursery. They may be able to help you or at least provide a good starting point.

Modi Green roof system from Green Innovations (*www.greeninnovations.ca*) sells units that are made from 100 percent recycled plastic. Stable, practical, and easy to assemble, any skilled worker can lay 250 square feet in under an hour. This system provides high water-proofing protection due to the staggered layout of the Modi's feet which have large, circular, support surfaces.

Green Tech (*www.greentechitm.com*) sells a residential product made of 100 percent recycled material that is simple to maintain and repair. An interlocking system makes installation easy and fast to customize. The material is lightweight, but sturdy with a fifteen-year guarantee.

Eco Star Nova (*www.ecostar.carlisle.com*) walkway mats are made from 100 percent recycled, post-industrial rubber and plastic. These pads provide a nonabsorbent, skid-resistant walkway for roof decks. The open grid design prevents water pooling. They are durable and should last for a very long time.

Invisible Products' Draincore conveyance layer (*www.invisibleproducts.com*) is used for advanced green roof applications as a replacement for antiquated French

Soil Retention Modules

drains. Draincore is a high volume drainage layer capable of withstanding heavy loads while allowing air and water transference for healthy turf and vegetation.

Exterior Solar Lighting

Solar lights need ample sunlight to charge during the day and work best when they are placed away from other lights. Solar lights come in all types including hanging lanterns, wall mounted security lights, and decorative sconces. Place solar lights along dark walkways and close to plants. If the project is in an area that isn't very sunny, purchase lights with additional solar panels and longer battery life. Solar lights usually need a few days to charge up, so wait a week after installation to see results.

If you decide to go with electricity-powered lights make sure to install motion detectors and timers so you are not wasting any additional electricity.

Patio Decks

Wood composite and recycled plastic lumber are my favorite choices for exterior decking. Wood-plastic composite lumber incorporates some of the characteristics of wood with plastic, which results in a product that more closely resembles traditional wood decking. Like plastic lumber, it will not rot, crack, or splinter but over time the color may fade. Recycled plastic lumber lasts forever, is maintenance free, doesn't require any toxic sealers and it removes plastic from the waste stream.

Choice Deck (*www.choicedeck.com*) is made with recycled wood fiber and recycled polyethylene plastic from items such as milk jugs and grocery sacks, keeping potentially unused waste out of landfills. This product is resistant to rot, decay, termite damage, and doesn't require any paints or stains.

For over twenty years Moisture Shield (*www.moistureshield.com*) has manufactured environmentally friendly deck material. Over the last decade they have been recognized with dozens of awards for their eco-friendly manufacturing and products. Their composite decks are made from 90 percent recycled materials like plastic bags, milk jugs, detergent bottles, and other pre- and post-consumer waste. They don't cut down new trees to make the product and their efforts have diverted over 270 million pounds of trash from entering landfills.

PREFAB HOMES

Prefab homes are the easiest and probably least expensive way to build green. Because these structures are prefabricated in controlled environments there is less construction site debris to address. The homes are erected on-site in a matter of hours instead of months or years. Increased quality, less waste, less money, and less time are the outcomes when you go the prefab route. In addition, the homes are stronger and more level than traditionally built homes.

Method Homes (*www.methodhomes.com*) is committed to sustainable design and construction. By building homes in their factory instead of on-site, they are able to reduce construction waste to less than 10 percent versus the 30 percent which is common with on-site construction. Method Homes come standard with enhanced insulation, solar power options and Energy Star appliances. The homes offer radiant heat, increased ventilation and no-VOC finishes or other harmful chemicals that contribute to indoor air pollution. Every Method home targets LEED for Homes 2.0 gold certification or higher.

Michelle Kaufman Designs (*www.mkd-arc.com*) is the leader in prefabricated, luxury eco-homes. Smartly designed with green materials, the homes are energy efficient, healthy for the environment and conserve water. They guarantee that their structures will achieve Gold or Platinum LEED ratings and they will work with home owners to qualify for Energy Star and other rating systems. The Web site has a lot of green information, blogs, videos, and a ton of green articles featuring Michelle.

Cargotechture is an architectural term coined by Seattle firm HyBrid (*www.hybridseattle.com*) for buildings made with shipping containers. I've seen these popping up all over the place over the last few years. I think they make great home offices, as it feels very industrious to work inside a shipping container, like you're really going somewhere.

IC Green's reclaimed shipping containers (*www.icgreen.net*) are the next breakthrough in housing and sustainable green structures. They are affordable, yet architecturally pleasing and range from a small backyard cabana to expansive residences.

Green Planet (*www.greenplanetbuilding.com*) is an L.A.-based construction firm that specializes in green building. What I like about this firm is their commitment to the planet and to people. For every green project they complete, they sponsor a child in the SOS Children's Village Program where 73,000 orphans are raised in 473 villages in 132 countries including the United States. With ten to fifteen homes in each village, six to ten children per home, this program is changing over one million lives. Like green home builders, SOS builds eco-sustainable homes and villages for their children. Many homes are built from natural, local materials in their area. Ask your contractor what they are doing about the environment and helping others.

GREEN BUILDING SITES

Green Building Supply (*www.greenbuildingsupply.com*) features natural and nontoxic building materials that are certified, safe, and environmentally friendly.

Building Green (*www.buildinggreen.com*) is a membership site that contains green news, building products, project case studies, and LEED certification information. You don't have to join to browse and read the multitude of sustainable information.

At Green Home Building (*www.greenhomebuilding.com*), a husband and wife team offer free information on natural building and green architecture.

Sustainable Sources (*www.greenbuilder.com*) includes a green building professionals directory, a green real estate section, a sustainable source bookstore, and a green calendar of events.

Oikos (*www.oikos.com/products.com*) features green products and a bookstore.

United States Green Building Council (*www.usgbc.com*) is an independent company committed to providing accurate, unbiased, and timely information designed to help building industry professionals.

Salvage Web is a Web site that links buyers and sellers of architectural salvage. The Web site allows individuals, dealers, and traders to buy or sell for free.

Build.Recycle.Net (*www.build.recycle.net*) features used building materials that are available for sale. There are also sections for buy, sell, and trade.

Energy Efficient Rehab Advisor (*www.rehabadvisor.pathnet.org*) was developed with funding from the United States Department of Housing and Urban Development. This Web site serves the community by providing information on how to improve energy efficiency in renovation, rehabilitation, and existing buildings.

If you've made it this far in the book, you realize that there is a significant, negative impact that the built environment makes on the natural environment and human health. Building green amounts to making the choice early in the design process to use materials and systems that are more environmentally sound and healthier for you, your clients, and your planet. Breakthroughs in building science, technology, and operations give design and building professionals the tools to create better performing structures—use them. Green homes can include a variety of proven energy-efficient features that contribute to improved quality and homeowner health, lower energy demand, and less air pollution. As a design professional, you have the privilege to be a force in helping to repair the damage we've done to the planet and our bodies. Every step we take in the right direction makes a difference. Working together with the entire building team from site selection to material installation to building maintenance will help to ensure that you've created a space that is not only beautiful but is also durable, energy-efficient, and healthy.

10 CLEANING AND MAINTAINING INTERIORS AND LANDSCAPES

The two major factors concerning cleaning and maintenance of interiors and landscapes are toxic products and waste. We've spent nine chapters learning how to design, build, and furnish properties in a more sustainable and healthy manner. To turn around and drench them in toxic products on a weekly basis would be counterproductive to the green foundation we've laid. By this point we also realize that landfill space is scarce and expensive. The less we throw away, the less we need to be concerned with poisoning our environment, finding new places to dump trash, and wasting valuable resources. Eco-friendly maintenance of the interior and landscape helps to reduce the negative aspects these activities have on the environment. This chapter will go into detail about green cleaning methods and products, recycling, hazardous waste disposal, and outdoor maintenance.

To ensure that the home you've designed is run properly after you have gone, it is always a good idea to make a maintenance binder with specific details about the home including: water, gas, and electrical supply shut off locations, how to operate automated and low voltage systems, and relevant information from this chapter.

START AT THE FRONT DOOR

Place good old-fashioned welcome mats at all the entries to the home. When I studied for the LEED exam, one of the techniques I learned about was using track off mats at the entries of buildings to reduce indoor pollution. While this is a great idea (and who doesn't love a nice welcome mat?), an even better option is to remove your shoes when you enter a residence. This simple act helps to reduce the amount of pesticides and chemicals that accumulate on the soles of our shoes and then get tracked all over our indoor space. Some people still look at you funny when you ask them to remove their shoes before entering a residence. A way to encourage people to perform this act without having to ask is to design for seating, shoe, and slipper storage near an entry to home. As more people become aware of green interior design, I have been asked to include these areas in most of the homes I design.

Something as simple as installing a bookcase by an entry transforms an otherwise chaotic shoe explosion into a civilized way to store shoes by the main entrance. The neatly stacked shoes are a gentle reminder to all who enter that, "We are a shoes-off type of residence."

Viva Terra's recycled flip-flop entry mat is a colorful way to introduce your eco-friendly home or business to all who enter.

CLUTTER

Fires are one of the most toxic events that can occur in a residence. Do everything you can to prevent fires including installing smoke detectors, replacing batteries as needed, and installing sprinklers. A less expensive and effective fire prevention technique is to avoid clutter. Make sure to remove clutter by anything hot that can ignite like ovens, furnaces, and space heaters. Less clutter also means less dust, which requires fewer cleaning products and less water. I'm not a big fan of collecting things. I generally see them as dust magnets. Open spaces allow for fresh air to circulate and this makes a room feel more inviting. If someone does have a collection, make sure it is displayed in a closed glass or lucite case/cabinet; this will help eliminate most of the dust that a collection can collect.

CLEANING SUPPLIES

Organic cleaners are made mostly of plant-based materials. Synthetic cleaners are often made from petroleum-based products. Petroleum-based products are toxic and when they are rinsed down the drain, they wind up in our waterways and oceans. If you like eating fish you may want to begin using nontoxic cleaning products.

Furniture and finish materials also contribute to poor indoor air quality, which negatively affects our health. Conventional cleaning products, reintroduced to the home on a weekly basis, however, may be the biggest culprits. There are thousands of chemicals used in American cleaning products and new ones added each year. It is impossible to keep track of them all. Frequently, the EPA doesn't test chemicals in these products for human safety.

Keeping a clean and green house doesn't have to be expensive or a bother. Many cleaning products are already in your house and ready to be used. Dr. Bronner's Castile Soap, baking soda, white vinegar, Murphy's Oil Soap, spray bottles, and hand towels can be your complete cleaning arsenal.

Sometimes it takes decades of proof that a product is deadly before it is removed from production in the United States. Currently there are thousands of harmful chemicals in conventional cleaners that are being used every day. Replacing toxic cleaners with healthier options might be one of the easiest ways to literally clean up our act.

When my sister had her first child, she was a bit overprotective, as most of us are when baby number one comes home. One day while visiting her, I watched her "clean" her kitchen sink in horror. Pouring bleach in the same place where she cleaned my niece's bottles seemed insane to me. When I asked her, "Why on earth are you doing that?" She replied, "To kill germs." She learned this from television ads. Advertisers will have you convinced that you need a different "extra-strength" product for every single task. They will scare you into thinking you need special disinfectants and antimicrobial soaps to kill germs. This simply isn't true. In fact with a few simple, natural ingredients you can have nontoxic cleaners that will work throughout the entire house. And P.S., antimicrobial soaps are dangerous. They kill good bacteria, like the kind that make septic tanks work, and help the "bad" bacteria develop stronger immunity.

There are many natural, nontoxic cleaning products on the market. If you're uncertain if something is okay to use check for this wording on packages: phosphate-free, vegetable-oil-based, no dyes, fragrance-free, biodegradable, nonpetroleum-based. If you can purchase these cleaners in a bulk size and refill smaller containers it saves the need to extract materials, manufacture, and then dispose of them.

Seventh Generation (*www.seventhgeneration.com*) is a leader in eco-friendly consumer products that uses its spheres of influence to inspire its partners, its industry, and the business community to embrace a model of business where economic and social growth merge.

Mrs. Meyer's (*www.mrsmeyers.com*) uses renewable resources derived from plants such as corn, olive, coconut, and soy. When they need to use synthetic sources they select environmentally safe choices. All of their products are biodegradable or are able to break down in nonharmful decomposition products. All packaging is made of recyclable materials and they do not test on animals. Plus, the stuff smells great!

Trader Joe's (*www.traderjoes.com*) now has over 300 stores throughout the United States, providing low-cost, high-quality green cleaning products including their own brand. If you don't like the way something works, take it back. They give you a refund, no questions asked.

Costco (*www.costco.com*) is a membership only store that has incredible prices on bulk eco-friendly cleaners. The bigger size you can buy, the more energy you will conserve.

Restore's entire line (*www.restoreproducts.com*) is made with nontoxic, natural ingredients, and the bottles can be refilled at any Restore Refill location. This is one of the smartest eco packaging systems I've seen. Since those plastic bottles last forever, why not use them forever?

Method (*www.methodhome.com*) products are inexpensive and available in many discount super stores. They contain biodegradable ingredients derived from plants and recycled content packaging, they use renewable energy in their manufacturing sites, and they offset their employee commuting and travel with carbon credits.

Martha Stewart's Clean line (*www.marthastewart.com*) offers fragrance-free, plant-based cleaning products. They work well and don't break the bank.

Country Save (*www.countrysave.com*) features biodegradable, inexpensive cleaning products packaged in recycled and recyclable containers.

Bona (*www.bona.com*) sells a wood floor cleaning system that is water-based, nontoxic and pH neutral. What I like about the "mop" is that in addition to being a great gentle everyday cleaning system, unlike a Swiffer-type product, the mop heads are not disposable and can be cleaned in the washing machine.

Forget antibacterial soaps and stick with these great smelling, eco-friendly brands. Mrs. Meyer's products make wonderful hostess gifts and Trader Joe's hand soap is affordable for everyday use.

Nat-ur (*www.nat-ur.com*) sells kitchen and yard trash bags made from resins, which are annually renewable, ecology sound substitutes for petroleum-based plastic products. They've replaced nearly 100 percent of the petroleum-dependant additives used in traditional plastics with bio-based materials such as corn, wheat, tapioca, and potato starch.

Twist (*www.twistclean.com*) sells a "Dish Dumpling" sponge, made of cellulose and agave, is biodegradeable, unlike polyurethane sponges.

As simple as it sounds, water, vinegar, baking soda, hydrogen peroxide, lemon, cheap vodka, vegetable oils, and rags from old towels, tee-shirts, diapers, and socks can take care of most of the cleaning needs throughout a home. Buying a few spray bottles for each concoction and a using these ingredients to clean will save the environment from having to deal with millions of plastic bottles from production to transportation to disposal.

Vinegar is a superpower when it comes to healthy cleaning. It has natural antibacterial properties so it works as a beneficial disinfectant. Vinegar will clean most surfaces, but do not use it on limestone or marble because it may dissolve them. Make sure that the vinegar you are using is not made from petroleum sources. There should be an identifying label that says "made from grain" on the bottle.

Baking soda is also an all around cleaner, which acts as a mild abrasive when mixed with water or an odor absorber when placed in the refrigerator, freezer, or bottom of a trashcan.

For the times when you need something a little bit stronger, I recommend Murphy's Oil Soap and Bon Ami Cleanser. Murphy's Oil Soap is a miracle cleaner and one of my all-time favorites. It gently cleans almost any surface and smells great. When you need super scrubbing power try Bon Ami cleanser, a great substitute for chlorine-based Ajax or Comet.

Any time you can skip water, rags, and cleaning products by using a vacuum to suck up dirt, do it. It will use less resources and energy.

BATHROOMS

White vinegar and baking soda are really all you need to clean a bathroom that has just been installed or remodeled. After dust and hair are wiped or swept up, vinegar and baking soda will do most of the work. If you don't like the smell of vinegar, don't worry, it doesn't smell after it dries.

Toilet bowls can be cleaned with two cups of white vinegar (sit for a few minutes) and baking soda and a good scrubbing.

For shiny faucets, wipe them down with vinegar, follow up with a clean rag and wipe on a drop of oil to keep them shiny longer. Mineral deposits on faucets can be removed by soaking a rag in vinegar and allowing it to sit on the faucets for an hour.

For rust on any porcelain—sinks, tubs, toilets—use vinegar on a rag to wipe off.

When you want to regain that out-of-the-box sparkle, cheap vodka will produce a reflective shine on any metal or mirrored surfaces. Vodka has no color or smell and is a lot less toxic than rubbing alcohol.

Clogs are usually caused by hair and grease. Preventing these items from going down drains will aid in the elimination of clogs in the first place. If you do get a clog, try pouring baking soda and vinegar down the drain followed by boiling hot water. If that doesn't work call a plumber to snake the drain. Do not use harsh chemical products, they are unnecessary and they are bad for your health, indoor air quality, the drains, and the aquatic life at the other end of their journey.

Instead of using artificial air fresheners, which release harmful VOCs into the air, place fragrant plants like lavender, mint, basil, or rosemary in the bathroom. A trick that always eliminates a stinky smell immediately is lighting a match. We have a box of matches in every bathroom in our home.

In addition to helping to eliminate bad smells, exhaust fans should be used when showering or bathing to prevent mold and mildew. Or, if you have a window in the bathroom, make sure to open it when the bathroom is steamy for mold and mildew prevention. Ventilate for about fifteen minutes after the bathroom has become steamy.

Practice water conservation in the room that uses the most fresh water in the house. Don't use the toilet as an ashtray or wastebasket. Turn off the water while brushing teeth, shaving, soaping. If cold water will do, avoid using hot water. And take shorter showers.

KITCHENS

Try to use the garbage disposal as little as possible by adding leftover food to a compost pail. If you do use your disposal, keep it clean with ice and a leftover lemon.

If the drain becomes clogged use the same trick as in the bathroom. Pour baking soda, white vinegar down the drain and, after a half hour, pour boiling hot water down the drain.

It uses less water to run a full load of dishes than hand washing them. Adding white vinegar in the rinse dispenser of the machine will make dishes sparkle and eliminate the need for a harsh chemical rinsing agent.

To wash the dishwasher, place a bowl with about two

cups of white vinegar in the bottom of the dishwasher and run it without any additional cleaner.

Don't put wood in the dishwasher. This means knives, bowls, and cutting boards. It will dry them out and they will crack and be destroyed. In this case, you will have to clean and dry these items by hand. Make sure to clean cutting boards in cold water—hot water sets in odors. Follow with a thin layer of inexpensive vegetable oil every fourth time they are washed.

The best advice on keeping sinks clean is wipe up food and sauces before they stain. Baking soda or Bon Ami combined with scrubbing action will clean the sink without damaging it.

This same advice is used for the stove and oven. Spills and splatters should be wiped up immediately after the hot surface cools. This will eliminate the need for harsh chemical cleaners to clean caked on substances. Never use oven cleaner. Most are made with a chemical called sodium hydroxide. In addition to being extremely dangerous to breathe, the noxious chemicals seep into the earth and waterways when rags or paper towels are cleaned or disposed. For extremely filthy grills, let them sit in a gallon of water and 1 cup of baking soda overnight.

If raw meat juice has contaminated a surface, spray it with vinegar followed by hydrogen peroxide for a non-harmful germ-killing solution.

Tomato paste is a gentle polish for copper pots. To remove tarnish, dip them in boiling vinegar and wipe dry with a cloth. A salt and lemon scrub works too.

To clean silver use nontoxic, biodegradable polish. If you can't find one, line a sink or bowl with aluminum foil and pour in boiling water and a few tablespoons each of salt and baking soda. Set for ten minutes and then remove and polish with a dry, soft cloth. Repeat if necessary. But be aware that you must hand wash these items forever after because they tarnish to a yellow color if cleaned in a dishwasher.

Clean coffee makers and tea kettles with vinegar and water. In coffee makers run a few cycles of vinegar water through the machine. To remove mineral build up from tea kettles, boil vinegar and water for a half hour and polish the outside with a baking soda and vinegar paste.

Use unbleached wax paper, which is biodegradable, instead of plastic wrap.

If you use paper napkins, buy recycled products and recycle in a compost pail. It's really best to use cloth napkins over and over and over and over again.

Skip paper towels for cleaning spills and opt for dishtowels.

Turn on vents when cooking to keep the house clean and smoke out of the lungs.

Follow these tips for conserving water:

Operate the dishwasher only with a full load.

Scrape, don't rinse dishes before they are loaded into the dishwasher.

Buy a water efficient dishwasher.

Don't run hot water to thaw food.

Store drinking water in the refrigerator instead of letting the water run to cool.

SURFACES

Countertops, windows, mirrors, and showers can be cleaned with a mix of equal portions of vinegar and warm water in a spray bottle. Add a few drops of tea tree oil or lavender for a fragrant smell.

Dust regularly. Doing so eliminates build up of allergens.

Sweep, vacuum, and mop floors weekly. Fill a basin or bucket with cold water, add the appropriate amount of cleaner, put rags in, wring them out until they are damp, and mop away. Change rags as they accumulate too much dirt. If you have a normal amount of traffic and the floors are being swept, vacuumed, and wet-mopped once a week, these rags shouldn't be too dirty.

For no-wax floors, mop with one cup of vinegar for every gallon of water. (On laminate wood, use a half-cup for every gallon.) If the manufacturer states you shouldn't use vinegar, then don't. Use Murphy's Oil soap instead.

For glazed tile and stone floors mop with a half-cup of baking soda to one gallon of water, wash and rinse.

Most new floors don't require wax. Their finishes are long lasting and protective. If you have an older floor that requires wax, begin with a clean floor and apply an organic wax. Less trafficked areas probably only require a small amount of wax once or twice a year. Areas that are seldom walked on (under the furniture, close to walls) probably only need waxing once every few years.

MOLD AND MILDEW

The key to preventing mildew and mold is good ventilation. If you do spot mildew attack it immediately with a spray made of two cups of water and 1/4 teaspoon each of tea tree oil and lavender. Shake first and spray everywhere. The oils will do the work for you, there's no need to wipe.

Mold can also be sprayed with straight white vinegar and wiped off. The use of a dehumidifier in humid climates can help to eliminate mold and mildew, keeping it out of the air and off of your things. In humid weather, empty the drip pan and wipe it clean daily. Once a week, clean the water bucket with a natural cleanser or a spray of white vinegar followed by a spray of hydrogen peroxide and wipe clean.

FURNITURE AND AREA RUGS

White canvas slipcovers are one of my favorite upholstery treatments. The fact that you can just toss them in the washer when they are dirty is a dream. Clean all light-colored fabrics—slip covers, towels, sheets, etc., with hydrogen- or oxygen-based bleaches instead of chlorine-based bleach. Chlorine has been tied to breast cancer and wreaks all kinds of havoc on marine life when it eventually winds up in the ocean.

Leather can be cleaned and oiled with liquid saddle soap. Leather furniture can be oiled with inexpensive vegetable oil.

Don't use artificial furniture polish. It contains flammable and toxic chemicals that might smell nice, but nonetheless are polluting the indoor and outdoor environment. Instead, use natural-based polishes or vegetable oil. Two parts olive oil and one part lemon make a healthy, pleasant-smelling polish.

Vacuum rugs once a week. Once a month, sprinkle them with baking soda—sweep it into the rug with a stiff broom and vacuum the baking soda. For heavy-duty cleaning, steam clean carpets with water, no solution needed. Treat animal protein stains, like vomit, feces, blood, or urine, by picking up solids, blotting excess liquid, covering with baking soda, and spraying white vinegar on it until it bubbles. Vacuum excess baking soda.

Gum erasers from the art supply store are made of natural rubber and are great for erasing "mistakes" on upholstery, wallpaper, matte painted walls, and rugs.

To clean bodily fluids, other than blood, on mattresses or furniture, remove any solids, dip a rag into water and vinegar, spot clean, pour baking soda on the area, let it dry, and vacuum the baking soda, repeat as needed.

To clean blood on mattresses or furniture, spot clean by dabbing a wet cloth with a small amount of dish cleaner and continue dabbing with the clean areas of the cloth until the blood is gone. If the blood stains, pour a teaspoon of hydrogen peroxide directly on the spot, wait five minutes, and then dab with a dry cloth.

LAUNDRY

Toxins in laundry detergent consist of petrochemicals including phosphates, naphthalene, or phenol. The waste water from the detergent causes lakes, streams, and the ocean to have build ups of toxins causing harm to aquatic life. Choosing natural, nonpoisonous products will keep your laundry clean without harming people, animals, and the planet.

Purchase biodegradable, nonpetroleum, phosphate-free, fragrance-, dye-, and chlorine-free laundry detergent. Do not use more than is absolutely necessary. Buy powder instead of liquid detergent. Liquid detergent is made mostly of water, which costs more money to transport and package.

Separate loads and only wash whites and extremely dirty loads with hot water.

Don't use bleach, it weakens fibers and has a negative effect when it reacts with other chemicals, forming toxic compounds that harm aquatic life. Oxygen-based bleaches or a few cups of vinegar help to boost a detergent's cleaning power.

For drying, use a clothesline when allowed and a drying rack when indoors. When air-drying laundry in a damp climate, fill shallow pans of garden lime help to absorb moisture. They can then be used in the garden when they are replaced every few weeks. Line drying in direct sun has the effect of a whitener without any chemicals. Don't line dry colors in direct sun; they will fade.

If you have to use a dryer, make sure it's an energy efficient model. Something as simple as cleaning the lint before each load will greatly improve efficiency.

Don't use traditional dryer sheets. They contain a laundry list of carcinogenic toxins that can cause damage to vital organs and the respiratory, reproductive, and central nervous systems. A far healthier solution is to use vinegar. One half-cup in the rinse cycle will soften clothes and help to eliminate static cling build up in the dryer.

Try to avoid purchasing fabrics that need to be dry cleaned. If you must dry clean fabrics, use an eco-friendly dry cleaner.

Green Earth Cleaning (*www.greenearthcleaning.com*) is a company that sells environmentally safe dry cleaning processes and products to over 1,400 dry cleaning stores throughout the world. They replaced petroleum-based solvents with liquid silica (sand) to create a gentle solution for cleaning fabrics. If your local dry cleaner is not offering eco-friendly methods, turn them on to Green Earth Cleaning.

TRASH AND RECYCLING

In the seventies people used to bring their bottles and cans back to the store for change. Now they just throw them away, even though in most states you pay an extra five or ten cents on each drink bottle you buy. I love to see resourceful people collecting these valuable materials from trash bins to bring them to a recycling plant. Eventually when we run out of space to bury our trash, everything will be made of something that was recycled, and it will be mandatory that every product be recycled or able to decompose.

Unfortunately, we are not there yet. The recycling logistics are still a puzzle we are trying to solve. Plastic is

Photo by Roi Yerushalmi

Seventh Generation dish soap has been around for years and does a great job on greasy dishes. Costco laundry detergent is earth friendly and comes in a container that should last you quite some time.

our biggest problem—it's in most nonedible, disposable consumer products, it never biodegrades, and far too much of it is not recyclable. Even though most of it has a recycle symbol on it, not every region recycles every plastic. It makes me sick every time I have a piece of plastic that can't be recycled and it winds up in the trash. I am thrilled when I see compostable plastics for dining and food wrappers. Thankfully these materials are being used more and more often. Try to buy products that contain plastic that can be recycled in your area.

What do the different numbers inside of the recycling symbol mean?

1. PETE (Plyethylene Terephtalate)
   uses: mouthwash, drinks, dish detergent, and ketchup bottles
   recycles into: luggage, fabric, footwear, carpeting, fiberfill for clothes, bedding, sleeping bags

2. HDPE (High-Density Polyethylene)
   Uses: drink jugs, detergent bottles
   Recycles into: carpet, clothing, plant pots, detergent bottles, coat hangers, video cases, drainpipes, floor tiles, fencing, plastic lumber, and road barriers

3. PVC (Polyvinyl Chloride)
   Uses: plumbing pipes, vinyl siding, flooring and windows, electrical wire insulation
   Recycles into: packaging, decking, paneling, mud flaps, flooring, speed bumps, floor mats

4. LDPE (Low Density Polyetheylene)
   Uses: flexible lids and bottles
   Recycles into: envelopes, garbage can liners, floor tiles, furniture, compost bins, trashcans, plastic lumber

5. PP (Polypropylene)
   Uses: packaging, fabrics, car parts
   Recycles into: auto battery cases, battery cables, brooms, ice scrapers, oil funnels, rakes, and pallets

6. PS (Polystyrene)
   Uses: styrofoam, containers, lids, cups, and bottles
   Recycles into: light switch plates, thermal insulation, egg cartons, foam packaging, carryout containers, spray foam insulation

7. Other: anything other than the previous six listed or a plastic with made of two or more of the previous
   Recycles into: plastic lumber and custom products

The EPA recommends waste prevention, recycling, and then disposal for solid waste. A large amount of household waste comes from food that is thrown into the trash. Instead of tossing it out, recycle it. You've probably heard the term composting. It's just the act of recycling food into nutrient rich soil enhancer. Compost is also made of yard clippings. Recycle them too. Use biodegradable bags for the kitchen and yard waste. If you have access to a yard, the compost can be used in the soil. In dense urban areas where yards are not common and one has no need for composted food waste, look for community gardens, botanical gardens, and farmers markets that accept donated food scraps. Compost material must be plant-based—no meat or bones please.

Something I never knew and learned from Ellen Sandbeck's *Green Housekeeping* book is that you need to recycle paper in a timely manner. If you do not, it will become browned, brittle, and no longer suitable for recycling.

Things you place into a recycling bin must be clean and lids, caps, and metal or plastic rings must be removed.

Don't store excess building materials. Get rid of them (donate, sell, or gift) because they evaporate, warp, and erode when they are not used for long periods. They then turn into trash.

If you receive a box filled with plastic peanuts, you can recycle them at Mail Boxes, Etc. and other box/shipping stores.

Photo by Roi Yerushalmi

A home recycling center really amounts to nothing more than a few receptacles for different items. The most common trio includes a can for waste (trash), recyclables (metals, papers, plastics), and compost (food). Check with your municipality on how your area segregates recyclable items.

HAZARDOUS WASTE

The name pretty much says it all, hazardous waste. Most municipalities have facilities to deal with toxic waste. Check the Internet for hazardous waste facilities in your area. Enter the name of your city or county followed by "hazardous waste drop off" to view a list of facilities. When you are transporting items to the facility, do not mix them together in one container. Mixing chemicals can result in an explosion or fire. Keep them in their original containers if you can.

List of hazardous products:

Prescription drugs

Paints (however once they dry completely you can throw them in the trash), solvents, thinners, strippers

Pool and spa chemicals

Fluorescent light bulbs

Batteries

Motor oil, antifreeze

Poisons and pesticides

Never pour hazardous materials down a drain, into gutters/storm sewers, into the trash, or on the ground. Properly disposing of hazardous waste helps to protect our waterways, ground water, and soil. Burning your own trash is even worse. When plastic (which is in almost all trash) is burned it releases dioxins. Waste facilities have high enough temperatures to eradicate dioxins, but individuals do not. It is also not safe to burn petroleum products, treated wood, or rubber.

Store all toxic chemicals far away from living spaces. Toxic chemicals such as paints, solvents, and cleaners are often stored in garages and basements. Make sure they are kept away from anything that can ignite flames. Encourage homeowners not to keep old chemicals in their homes, but to dispose of them at hazardous waste facilities.

If there are going to be toxic products in the home, make sure to keep the labels on them in case of accidental poisoning. The list of ingredients may need to be conveyed to poison control.

Don't idle the car in a garage that is attached to a house. When the car has started, leave the structure and turn it off as soon as the vehicle enters the garage.

Use rechargeable batteries. When they die or if you have dead disposables, dispose of or recycle them properly.

Although attractive from an energy conservation standpoint, fluorescent bulbs have mercury and are extremely toxic when improperly disposed of. Always bring them to an appropriate facility. (One more thing to love about Ikea—they have a cool recycling bin at all of their stores for batteries and fluorescent bulbs.)

Have furnaces cleaned by a professional at the beginning of the heating season.

Don't use the fireplace with the damper closed—carbon monoxide will fill the room. I was having a romantic glass of wine with a boyfriend one evening and we didn't realize the damper was closed. We passed out from the carbon monoxide and thankfully were woken up by the fire department before we died. Don't learn the hard (embarrassing) way.

Electronics can be extremely hazardous when put into landfills. Check out the International Association of Electronics Recyclers (*www.iaer.org*). Ask about the recycling program of the manufacturer when you purchase an electronic item.

Apparently used ink jet cartridges and old cell phones are pretty valuable. There are many Web sites you can visit to collect cash for recycling these items. A few even have fundraising projects for nonprofit organizations. I'd much rather give school kids my old cartridges and cell phones than buy another roll of overpriced wrapping paper!

(*www.empties4cash.com*, *www.fundingfactory.com*, *www.inkjetcartridges.com*)

www.lamprecycle.com refers you to other sites with information about a hazardous materials/recycling center in your area.

Earth911 (*www.earth911.org*) locates a hazardous materials/recycling center near you.

OUTDOOR

Sometimes people think if they do something and everyone else doesn't, it just won't make a difference. So why bother? I recently experienced this very attitude on a project I'm working on that has a large hillside area that needs to be landscaped for two reasons. First, it's not attractive because it's a barren dirt hill. Second, when it rains, it becomes a potential landslide situation since there are no plant or tree roots to keep the dirt stable. The first thing the landscaper wanted to do was poison the hillside with toxic chemicals to kill all of the weeds before he planted. I asked him to consider an alternative because these chemicals were sure to run off the hill during watering into the street and make their way into the ocean. He responded by telling me that one hillside wouldn't make a difference. This is where people's thinking is wrong. That same landscaper has many properties, including golf courses and resorts, that he is responsible for amounting to thousands of square feet where he can stop using toxic pesticides and fertilizers. So he, alone, can make a difference in what he buys and uses. By buying more organic products, he can support the movement that makes organic products more readily available and affordable. He also has the opportunity to keep the toxins off of his projects and to let people know what he is doing and why. Sometimes when you do the right thing, it becomes contagious. When others learn how easy and affordable it is to be green, they are more than willing to try these same actions.

Just this morning I saw a story on CNBC discussing that Scott's, one of the world's leading fertilizer and pesticide companies, was starting to sell a natural line made with soybeans instead of petrochemicals. They were doing this because they didn't want to be left behind in the environmental revolution the way Kodak Film was left behind when digital cameras became popular. So see, voting with your green dollars works!

What's the big deal about synthetic pesticides, fertilizers, and herbicides, anyway? For decades harmful chemical pesticides, fertilizers, and herbicides have been used all over the world making most of the farmland soil unhealthy. When soil is treated with synthetic pesticides, fertilizers, and herbicides, the organic matter (earth worms and microorganisms) is killed. These toxic chemicals also make the soil dry, which requires more of our precious fresh water supply to irrigate these crops. Soil with thriving organic matter pulls down carbon dioxide, which is digested by the microorganisms. This greatly reduces global warming. It also allows the organic matter to fertilize the soil, making it moist, healthy, and mineral-rich for the next crop.

In order to eliminate the need for artificial pesticides and fertilizers, plant native species of flowers, grasses, trees, and shrubs. They will thrive in their natural climates, requiring less water, pesticides, fertilizers, and herbicides. This is because native species have adapted to pests in their climates.

Because composting encourages microorganisms to thrive resulting in healthier soil, use it as a soil enhancer in place of fertilizer. Include a mix of brown (wood chips and straw) materials and green materials (kitchen scraps, lawn cuttings, leaves). If you need fertilizer, only use an organic variety once before the start of the growing season.

Don't use synthetic pesticides. Remove dead or diseased leaves immediately and spray with an organic pesticide (or a crushed, strained garlic water spray) to keep disease from spreading. Remember that not all bugs are bad. Nematodes, ladybugs, and spiders are very happy to eat unwanted visitors. Spiders might be scary but they sure do eat their fair share of pests. Beer, vinegar, and ducks are your first line of organic defense against snails. Beer attracts the slugs, then they drown and the ducks find them very tasty. That good old vinegar spray also kills the slugs on contact. Throw the dead ones in the compost pile.

Kill weeds with vinegar spray, boiling water, or crushed rock salt. Use mulch very close to the bottom of plants to deter weeds from sprouting.

Mulch can also be placed on top of soil to help retain moisture (less need for watering) and reduce weeds (less need for herbicides). Mulch can be made of bark, wood chips, leaves, grass clippings, and pine needles and will need to be replaced every year because it breaks down into the soil. Around vegetable gardens you can mulch worn out, used carpet that was made of natural materials (that's one way to keep it out of the landfill).

When fighting insects, a small pond filled with insect eating fish is a much better solution to mosquito problems than chemical-laden citronella candles.

Create a rain garden. This is a small area of the yard that is at a lower level than the rest of it (four to five inches will work). When it rains or snows the rain garden will collect the water allowing it to percolate into the soil instead of causing soil erosion or storm water runoff into the waterways.

Lawns are not an eco-friendly feature of an outdoor space. If you insist on having a grass lawn, consider a manual push mower or efficient electric and propane mowers/trimmers, not gas-powered ones. There are also solar powered, self-moving machines on the market.

Clean gardening tools with vinegar and steel wool and store in a dry place or in sand. Keep tools sharp for better, easier cuts.

Don't waste water. Hoses should have trigger nozzles so they don't waste water while washing down patios or watering potted plants. Place water barrels under drain spouts and use the water for patio plants.

Use only biodegradable, chlorine- and phosphate-free products when cleaning your outdoor areas. This will prevent toxic water from running into waterways and the soil.

To clean decks and outdoor furniture, spray with water, sprinkle baking soda all over the surface, work with a long handled scrub brush or a hand held scrub brush, wait fifteen minutes, and rinse.

Make sure pools have a cover that keeps them clean and requires the use of fewer chemicals. Or, better, switch to saltwater pools.

Resources

- *www.nl-amer.com*—organic-based lawn care
- *www.cleanairgardening.com*—manual and electric lawn mowers, composting bins, rain barrels
- *www.composters.com*—composting bins
- *www.extremelygreen.com*—organic products
- *www.natural-insect-control.com*—beneficial insects, traps, and barriers
- *www.groworganic.com*—tools and supplies for organic gardeners
- *www.planetnatural.com*—garden and home supplies
- *www.seedsofchange.com*—organic seeds
- *www.urbangardencenter.com*—compost bins and recycled outdoor furniture
- *www.southface.org*—guide to rainwater collection
- *www.organicgardening.com/steps*—ways to garden without toxic pesticides
- *www.gardensablaze.com/companions.htm*—a guide of which plants to place near each other to help with pest control
- *www.recycleworks.org/compost/pooppat.htm*— what cannot be added to compost piles
- *www.gardensalive.com*—organic herbicides, pesticides, fertilizers, environmentally responsible products
- *www.groworganic.com*—organic growing supplies, natural fertilizers, organic pest control, and organic seeds
- *www.wormsway.com*—a wide selection of gardening products including worms for your compost bin

11 MY FAVORITE GREEN DESIGNERS, ARCHITECTS, AND BUILDERS

Designers all over the country have gone green, creating healthy environments that tread a little lighter on our planet. This chapter focuses on the designs of some of the best and most accomplished green designers, architects, and builders in business today. With a wide spectrum of styles from ultra modern to extremely traditional, there are plenty of examples of unique and interesting ways to incorporate sustainable materials and lifestyles into beautiful, functional spaces.

Whether you like it or not, change is coming. A world consciousness regarding our actions and their effect on the environment has been ignited, as evidenced by the Copenhagen Climate Conference in December 2009. After a week of careful examination, a voluntary treaty of many nations to reduce their carbon footprints resulted. Since 30 percent of the waste stream is coming from the building industry, it seems reasonable that the course of action many governments will take to accomplish these goals will be mandatory codes enforcing green methods of building. Combine this collective desire to control greenhouse gases with the fact that there are limited resources and expensive energy costs in our near future as the world population

Polished concrete floors, which keep this South Florida home cool during the day and warm at night, were used in the living room.

Incandescent lighting was replaced throughout the home with Osram's Decostar Energy Saver halogen light bulbs. They are 30 percent more efficient than incandescent and have a five year lifespan. Halogen bulbs do not contain the mercury found in compact fluorescents.

continues to grow and it's hard to come to any other conclusion. Local and state governments around the country are enforcing green mandates concerning appliances, lighting, and construction. Los Angeles County has already mandated that 5 percent of all construction demolition be sorted for recycling or resale, and the state of California will not allow a lamp or light fixture to be sold without a fluorescent bulb included in the package. China is enforcing all sorts of environmental laws regarding construction, and Europe has been doing this for years.

This puts designers, builders, and architects who have acquired the valuable skill set of eco-friendly practices in great demand in the coming years. It will also place those who did not learn these conservation methods at a disadvantage. This is probably why I am seeing standing room only at green design lectures that were half empty a few years ago.

Enjoy the following projects and think about the ways in which these designs are similar to your own and the ways in which they are different. My hope is that their work will inspire you to take what you've learned in this book and transform your practice and our world.

PORT ST. LUCIE, FLORIDA, HOME BY SUSAN COZZI, ALLIED ASID

The home is twenty-five years old, and in addition to being "dated" it was not functional and desperately needed updating. The first step of the remodel was contacting a green demolition company in an effort to reuse as many

In the master suite, bamboo flooring was used. It is a renewable, fast-growing fiber and a material that acclimates well to a humid climate. This was especially important because this homeowner prefers opens windows to air conditioning. Bamboo was also used for the entertainment wall in the living room.

Rooms by Susan Cozzi, photos by Michiko Kuriso

materials and fixtures as possible. Unwanted items were then donated or sold to keep waste out of landfills.

In the bedroom, the headboard is made from a reclaimed piece of wood and hand made by a vendor who specializes in reclaimed wood furniture.

About Susan Cozzi, Allied ASID

Susan received her degree in Interior Design from FIT in New York City and is an Allied Member of the American Society of Interior Designers. Her work was recently featured in two books, *Residential Design for Aging in Place* and *The Green Home: A Sunset Design Guide*. She is a public speaker on sustainable design throughout the East Coast.

Susan Cozzi Design Studio
1200 Ocean Blvd
Boca Raton, FL 33432
www.cozzidesign.com

Accessories and art were purchased at local and state craft fairs supporting local artisans and the community.

Rooms by Kati Curtis, photos by Gregory Holm

CENTRAL PARK, NEW YORK HOME BY KATI CURTIS, ASID, LEED AP

This New York apartment overlooking Central Park has small, enclosed spaces. The homeowners wanted to open the space up and take advantage of the views. Initially they were not interested in green design, but that changed with Kati's gentle coaching and the news that a baby was on the way. Halfway through the design process they began to see value in the green designs that were being implemented. The lack of toxic smell in the paint and cabinets helped to illustrate the healthy environment Kati was creating for them. The clients, being nervous new parents, were thrilled to learn about the antimicrobial qualities of their CaesarStone countertops, especially now that sterilization of bottles was to become part of their daily routine. Slowly but surely by the completion of the warm, modern renovation, Kati's clients became green converts.

Green elements include:

Benjamin Moore Aura paint

Old kitchen cabinets recycled and used by contractor for another project

Energy Star rated kitchen appliances

Urea-formaldehyde-free, FSC-certified wood cabinet boxes finished with acrylic-based, low-VOC lacquer

Recycled glass tile backsplash

CaesarStone countertops

Incandescent lighting replaced with compact fluorescents or halogen bulbs

Vintage furnishings upholstered in Crypton Green Fabric which is Cradle to Cradle certified

Organic cotton bedding

Bedroom window treatments and upholstery in Carnegie 100 percent recycled polyester

Wool carpets

About Kati Curtis, ASID, LEED AP

Before forming Nirmada in 2004, Kati worked with architects in Washington, DC, San Francisco, Los Angeles, and New York. Her work has been featured in *USA Weekend*, *The Wall Street Journal*, and on BobVila.com. Her projects have received nationwide recognition including the International Design Association's Silver Award and the Army Corps

Rooms by Kati Curtis, photos by Gregory Holm

of Engineers Design Award for adaptive reuse and preservation of the National War College in Washington, DC. She gives back by teaching at Parsons School of Design in New York and volunteering for Design Industry Foundation for AIDS and the Thorn Tree Project in conjunction with Clodagh Cares. She currently serves on the Board of Directors for the New York chapter of ASID. You can learn about her daily design experiences in her blog.

Nirmada
205 West 54th Street 4G
New York, NY 10019
www.nirmada.com

Sand Point, Long Island home by Jamie Gibbs and Associates

RESIDENCES BY JAMIE GIBBS

In every residence he designs Jamie Gibbs executes three green Rs: repair, recycle, reclaim. He uses antique furnishings, artwork, and light fixtures. He recycles old carpets and reconfigures old drapery treatments. Reupholstering and slip covering fine pieces of furniture is a regular practice for in his projects as well as refurbishing fixtures for kitchens and baths.

City Home by Jamie Gibbs

This 1912 apartment was completely restored using reclaimed materials, antiques, and accessories. All of the architectural details are new to these rooms, but come from antique sources. The Wood-Mode kitchen cabinets and tin ceilings are reclaimed from another apartment.

City home by Jamie Gibbs

City home by Jamie Gibbs and Associates

Old Westbury Home by Jamie Gibbs

This estate was built in 1922 and was recently restored. Antiques and reclaimed or refurbished materials make up this splendid estate. The only new things in this home are mattresses, linens, and labor.

Lenox, Massachusetts, Home by Jamie Gibbs

This restored mansion, down the street from a home Edith Wharton once owned, is the summer residence for the conductor of the Boston Pops. During the Tanglewood Festival it is used for nightly dinners and receptions. The dining chairs are stacking, recycled cafeteria chairs covered in artificial moss.

Sand Point, Long Island, Home by Jamie Gibbs

The original library of this grand house is now the great room for the twelve condos that have been reconfigured from the original residence. This clever reuse of space allows for the design of smaller individual spaces and the sharing of a community area.

About Jamie Gibbs

Jamie Gibbs attended Purdue and Columbia Universities, where he studied architecture, landscape architecture, horticulture, historic preservation and the decorative arts at both the undergraduate and graduate levels. He holds five degrees with extensive continuing studies. His work has been featured in many shelter magazines and newspapers such as *The Wall Street Journal*, the *New York Times*, *House Beautiful*, *Woman's Day*, *Traditional Home*, *Design Times*, *Forbes*, *House and Garden*, *Old House Interiors*, *Garden Design*, and industry publications. He has authored two design books and has been featured in over thirty hardcover books. Mr. Gibbs also sat on the editorial board at Grace Publishing for over ten years and has been an adjunct professor at Parsons School of Design since 1988. In December of 2002 and 2003,

City home by Jamie Gibbs and Associates

Mr. Gibbs was an "Honored Visiting Professor" at the International Design School in Moscow, Russia. In 2005, Mr. Gibbs created the dining room décor for the ASID Scarsdale Show House. He lectures on all things design throughout the United States.

Jamie Gibbs and Associates
122 East 82nd Street
New York, NY 10028
www.jamiegibbsassociates.com

SULLIVAN'S ISLAND, SOUTH CAROLINA, HOME BY STEPHEN HERLONG

Located on Sullivan's Island, a coastal barrier island near Charleston, SC, this home overlooks the creeks and marshes that identify the Carolina Low Country. This property had a small but unremarkable residence on the site that was considered a liability by the realtors and was listed as a teardown. The owners decided instead on a more ecologically friendly approach of relocating the existing house to an interior lot on the island and renovating it, and then designing the new energy-conscious home on the waterfront property.

This community has addressed its growing concern that oversized, disproportionate homes are changing the unique character of the island by limiting the size and footprint of homes and by increasing the building setbacks. This home compliments the community by placing its smallest component, a simple one and one half story bedroom wing, on the street-side façade. The opposite façade is, in fact, the front façade as it addresses the open expanse of marsh and harbor vistas. This water façade is tall and transparent to provide three stories of living space with dramatic views of the coastal marshes and waterways. The adjacent property has a historic boathouse clad in weathered cedar shingles. The dark stained shingles on the upper level are in harmony with the boathouse, while the white siding on the lower level gives a nod to the turn-of-the-century island cottages that dot the island.

This home is very personal in that it is a culmination of the owners' experiences. Having grown up in the rural South, they recognize the sense of community the streetscape can create. The owners wanted the street-side

façade represented as a simple gabled structure—visually appealing, comfortable in scale, and unimposing. The owners also have strong ties to the water, having lived aboard boats and sailed across the Atlantic. The "lighthouse" represents the most welcoming symbol a sailor will ever see. Stylistically, the lighthouse is derived from images of the first octagonal wooden lighthouse on Sullivan's Island, lost more than a century ago to a hurricane.

About Stephen Herlong

Stephen Herlong is owner and principal of Herlong & Associates. Not many people determine their future profession in the sixth grade, and even fewer people pursue and excel in that profession. But that's exactly how Steve Herlong landed in the field of architecture.

Riding bikes with his friends, the young Herlong spotted a house barely visible through the trees. The creek seemed to run almost under the house and it was finished in all natural wood. When Herlong asked him mom about the house, she told him an architect lived there and had designed it for his family. At that moment, Herlong knew he was going to be an architect and design interesting homes.

Herlong went to Clemson University, graduating in 1979 with a Bachelor of Arts in design. He launched his career at an award-winning commercial architecture firm before serving as president of a successful design-build firm focused on custom homes.

But after thirteen years, Herlong wanted something more from his architectural career. He and his wife,

The first elevated level provides for the functional spaces of bedrooms, the entry hall, and dual home office spaces.

In lieu of extensive upper porches that expand the building footprint, the owners utilized the inherent ground level space to create comfortable, easily accessible living and entertaining spaces. The materials used are classic and timeless, built to withstand the sands of time and delight for generations. The house was featured in the April 2009 issue of *Coastal Living* magazine in a feature on living green at the beach.

Warren Lieb, Photography provided by Herlong & Associates

In keeping with the owners' program requirements, the upper floor holds the living and cooking areas with striking views of the marshes and waterways.

A registered architect in South Carolina since 1984, Herlong has designed award-winning homes throughout the Charleston area, the barrier islands of South Carolina, and other coastal regions. Herlong serves on the board of the American Institute of Architects in Charleston and is the vice chairman of the Sullivan's Island Design Review Board. Herlong is an active member of the Congress of Residential Architects and the Custom Residential Architects' Network.

Stephen Herlong & Associates, Inc.
103 Palm Blvd Ste. 3-A
Isle of Palms, SC 29451
www.herlongarchitects.com

Warren Lieb, Photography provided by Herlong & Associates

Susan, loaded up their thirty-seven-foot cutter-rigged sailboat and embarked on a three-year sailing adventure throughout Europe and the Mediterranean. The experience left Herlong filled with inspiration and an intense understanding of how being connected to nature impacts the quality of life.

His passion for architecture revived, Herlong founded Herlong & Associates, a firm that makes a connection to nature a founding principle of its design work. Located on the Isle of Palms, Herlong & Associates is situated on a barrier island between the Atlantic Ocean and the Intracoastal Waterway. The third-floor offices have an abundance of windows, a reminder of the importance of infusing nature into the firm's design work.

Charleston is the perfect setting for Herlong's firm. With the water, open spaces, and marshes, nature is all around. Building custom homes primarily along the waterfront, Herlong & Associates takes great care to maximize the views, the natural light, and the sounds of the water.

GREEN BEACH HOUSE BY KEITH MILLER

This home was built as a green demonstration project, meeting standards for:

Energy Star, American Lung Association Health House, LEED for Homes (Gold), Environments for Living, The National Association of Home Builder Green Certification, and Master Builders Association of King & Snohomish Counties Five Star Built Green. The goal was to craft a home that reflected the taste and style of the

Stairwell by Keith Miller, photo by Northwest Property Imaging

Room by Keith Miller, photo by Northwest Property Imaging

homeowner while blending in with beach neighborhood. The owners and builders were deeply concerned with creating an awareness within the building and consumer communities about green building and design.

The 100-year-old beach cabin, situated on a narrow lot (32 feet by 125 feet), is located in a sensitive marine environment. The owners wanted as much living space as possible without over building. By planning space efficiently (think boat design) they were able to achieve their goal of living "large" in a small footprint. The home is all about sustainability, from design to interior furnishing. It is built following Cradle to Cradle principles and designed following Universal Design principles with its wider doorways, curbless shower, pedestal sink, hard surface flooring, and lowered light switches.

With the help of a green construction expert many sustainable practices were incorporated from

Recycled glass was used by local artists to create a stunning, fanciful chandelier over the kitchen island and a dramatic and enchanting breakfast bar countertop.

the point of deconstruction (80 percent was salvaged or recycled) to the advanced framing techniques. The shell is sided with long-lasting cement fiberboard which was faux painted to resemble cedar shakes. The metal roof has a fifty-year life. The home is heated with geothermal in-floor radiant heat throughout. Cooling is provided by low energy ceiling fans, sun-blocking shades, a mechanized awning, and operable windows in the cupola. Windows and insulation provide the high energy efficiency. Indoor air quality is enhanced by only hard-surface flooring—FSC-certified hardwoods, cork, bamboo, lead-free tile or stone and linoleum—low- or no-VOC paints, finishes and adhesives; and GreenGuard-certified window coverings.

Many furnishings are made from recycled or sustainable materials or are salvaged pieces.

Salvaged materials from the original cabin (such as yellow pine paneling shown in the bathroom cabinetry) and from other sources (such as the Alaskan marble island counter) save natural resources while giving the home a venerable feel.

including LEED Gold, the home feels as relaxed and playful as a day at the beach.

About Keith Miller

Keith Miller greatly appreciates just about every style of design and prefers to create a client's personal fashion, rather than imposing his own signature style. He's a chameleon that way. He is passionate about green interior design and aims to share his knowledge with people throughout the world.

Miller Interior Design
2033 Second Avenue #1208
Seattle, WA 98121
www.millerinteriordesign.com

Geothermal and solar power, radiant floors, and windows with mechanized awnings combine energy efficiency with cozy comfort and stunning views. Creative use of the thirty-foot-wide lot allows terraced gardens and space for entertaining, while a vegetated roof and pervious concrete protect Puget Sound by filtering stormwater runoff.

Many rooms serve a dual purpose but leave plenty of space for entertaining, exercising, and quiet reflection. The exercise room doubles as a craft/workshop space. The flat walls of the stairwell were replaced with built-in bookcases and art display shelves. The cupola provides natural light and 360-degree view of the ocean, mountains, and islands. Despite its impressive green credentials,

The massive fireplace surround is fabricated from local rock off the beach.

MANHATTAN BEACH, CALIFORNIA, HOME BY DANIEL SALZMAN

Daniel's goal with this home was to create an environment that is warm, practical, and conducive to creativity and energy—a home that allows one to breathe and think clearly.

Green features include:

LED lighting that uses 1/12 of the energy of incandescent and 50 percent of CFL with no mercury and dimmable bulbs that last up to twenty-five years

Solar PV panels that power 60 percent of the energy bill

Demand hot water system with tankless water heaters

Greywater system that feeds underground drip irrigation

Native, drought-tolerant landscaping and herb garden, fed by drip irrigation

Native, drought-tolerant landscaping and herb garden, fed by drip irrigation

LED landscape lighting

Three types of green insulation (recycled cotton, recycled dry cellulose, blown-in foam)

All stain, paints, glues, and sealers are no- or low-VOC. A garage exhaust fan turns on when the garage door closes to dissipate carbon monoxide

House has radon venting underneath the foundation that vents all the way through the roof

Built-in automatic composter in the kitchen

Mud room bench for removing shoes in entry, with built-in

©Evergreen Design Build, Inc., room by Daniel M. Salzman

vacuum in base of cabinet to clean dirt off shoes

Programmable lighting system with dim settings

Shingles on exterior have rain screen technology to help moisture evaporate quickly

Framed structure was pre-treated during framing stage with nontoxic borate to repel termites

Concrete foundation has high level of fly-ash in composition (30 percent)

Basement dehumidifer

Super-efficient, three-stage filtration forced air units with programmable thermostats

Energy Star appliances, ventilation fans, windows, skylights, and roof sheathing

FSC American walnut floors

Natural cooling tower that draws cool basement air to upper levels via automatic operable skylights

About Daniel M. Salzman

Daniel is an artistic builder who came to green design and building because the philosophies and science behind a high-performance home, along with the innovative use of recycled and reclaimed finish materials, go hand in hand with creating a healthier and more efficient lifestyle. He is a "method builder," approaching every project as if it were his own so he can visualize how the home will be lived in, from its practical and thoughtful details to its innovative and technological needs. While he enjoys working on all building styles, he is drawn to fresh interpretations of traditional styles with a modern feel in the finishes and lighting, so the homes feel comfortable and familiar but new at the same time.

Salzman Design Build Inc.
PO Box 3730
Manhattan Beach, CA 90266
www.salzmandesignbuild.com

©Evergreen Design Build, Inc., room by Daniel M. Salzman

Designed for natural light and ventilation

Water Sense toilets and low-flow aerators on faucets

Bathroom by Barbara Treves, photo by Derek Rath

Eco-friendly features in this bathroom include: CaesarStone counters, recycled glass tile, bamboo cabinets, dual flush toilet, low-flow shower and faucets, a Metland hot water pump that circulates hot water as needed, an operable skylight for ventilation, and natural light and motion sensors for lights.

VENICE, CALIFORNIA, HOME BY BARBARA TREVES

Completed in January 2009, 1301 Preston Way in Venice, California, is one of only six LEED Platinum certified residences in all of Los Angeles County. The open plan, three bedroom home was designed and constructed following the highest building standards and using superior fabrication techniques as well as intelligent innovation and design. Advanced energy systems such as radiant floor heating, solar PV, solar thermal, Energy Star products, and water saving technologies in the form of dual flush toilets, low-flow showerheads, and rain catchment systems were all seamlessly combined to create an environment that expresses a new consciousness for residential buildings. The sustainable integrity of the home is carried through the material and finish selections. In order to maintain the pristine indoor air quality, Greenguard-certified CeasarStone was selected for all counter tops, low-VOC paints and nontoxic plasters completed the wall finishes, and concrete and bamboo flooring were selected over carpeting, which tends to harbor dirt and dust.

In the six months since its opening, Preston Way has served as an educational tool, not only for the general

Eco features include bamboo floors, radiant heating, no-VOC paint.

Bedroom by Barbara Treves, photo by Derek Rath

The open floorplan living-dining room has the same type of cabinetry used in the kitchen, but configured to house an entertainment system, accessories, and books. Materials include rift-sawn oak veneer cabinets over a green-rated, formaldehyde-free, and recycled content substrate.

Residents keep warm by the fire in this example of how to design the perfect indoor outdoor space. The exterior fixtures are fluorescent.

Living room by Barbara Treves, photo by Derek Rath

public but also for developers and city building officials who will no doubt be incorporating some, if not all, of these new building standards into future projects creating homes that not only serve the best interests of homeowners but of the planet as well.

About Barbara Treves, LEED AP

Born in Toronto, Canada, Barbara exhibited a penchant for the visual arts from a very early age. Training in textile design and photography at the Ontario College of Art led

A beautiful view from the second floor.

Design by Barbara Treves, photos by Derek Rath

her to a career in fashion design, which included working for such notable companies as St. John Knits and Leon Max, eventually launching her own successful import and manufacturing company in 1989. The company grew to include such notable clients as Neiman Marcus, Saks Fifth Avenue, Nordstrom Department Stores, and Bergdorf Goodman.

While the world of fashion taught Barbara a great deal about the way design and materials affect a finished garment, she was drawn to the greater challenge of applying those learned concepts to the built environment and so began the path toward a second career as an interior designer.

While attending evening classes at Santa Monica College, Barbara accepted a position at the well-respected interior design firm of

In the lounge, bamboo floors and solar thermal radiant heating floors, no-VOC paints and passive solar light and heat are key eco features.

In the Xeriscape landscaping, drip irrigation, raised gardens filled with organic soil, solar roof panels, fluorescent lighting on timers, and rainwater barrels (to replenish aquifers) were some of the ways the designer made this exterior sustainable and a place where you want to spend time.

Design by Barbara Treves, photos by Derek Rath

These planters not only look good, but are also easier to retrieve edible plants from because they're raised. They're also filled with organic soil.

Renewable fibers make up the exterior day bed. Relaxing in the fresh air renews the spirit and gives you an opportunity to soak up your daily dose requirement of vitamin D.

Polished concrete floors with 25 percent fly ash content, solar thermal radiant floors, and no-VOC paint helps to make this home office an attractive, healthy, and productive place to work.

Darrell Schmitt Design Associates. Eventually earning an honors degree in interior architectural design, her position within the firm advanced quickly to that of senior designer on such projects as the recent remodeling of the guest suites at the Hotel Casa del Mar in Santa Monica, CA.

Barbara is passionate about education and continually upgrades her skills and knowledge base, especially as it pertains to the environment. She recently earned LEED AP designation from the United States Green Building Council and is committed to applying sustainable building principals to future projects.

The house on Preston Way in Venice, California, was her first independent LEED project and Barbara is very proud to have helped it earn the highest rating of Platinum.

Barbara Treves, LEED AP
12737 Westminster Ave.,
Los Angeles, CA 90066
(310) 390-6891
trevesbarbara@yahoo.com

This is the front entry to the home. The building was placed on the site to take maximum advantage of passive solar light and heat. The designer was careful to include "walk-off" mats at the entry to help remove dirt and contaminants before entering the home.

© Westlake Design Studio

The sophistication of the antique carpet and wine table pair nicely with the rustic, reclaimed wood dining table in this airy Craftsman dining room. The Craftsman style generally is dominated by dark wood paneling, which tends to absorb natural light like a sponge. Painting the prominent paneling in this room a light color allows more natural light to bounce around the room.

WOODBURY, GEORGIA, HOME BY KRISTI WESTLAKE, ALLIED ASID, LEED AP

Flooring is original to the house circa 1910. The harvest table is made from reclaimed barn wood (the barn was located on property and removed to make room for the pool area). The buffet is an Asian antique wine table.

Placing an antique Asian-style wine table in this Craftsman dining room is an unexpected treasure against the no-VOC painted, paneled wall.

© Westlake Design Studio

© Westlake Design Studio

MARIETTA, GEORGIA, HOME BY KRISTI WESTLAKE, ALLIED ASID, LEED AP

Not everyone can afford expensive furnishings and materials. Kristi Westlake illustrates how you can be green and chic on a tighter budget. Kristi's keen eye for vintage and antique items discovered at tag sales and flea markets shapes her interiors with eco-friendly individuality without depleting the planet's resources or her client's bank accounts.

This home office is affordable, easy to install, and designed with sustainable materials. The conference table is made from reclaimed cypress, mahogany, and bamboo. The chairs are made from recycled aluminum. The desk and hutch are made from bamboo. The flooring is reclaimed pine finished with a natural nontoxic finish. The lighting fixtures are Energy Star rated. The wall paint is a zero VOC paint. The curtains are hand made organic linen. The picture frames and matte are made from recycled materials.

Kristi Westlake makes the most of the limited space she has by carving out a niche to create a welcoming workspace. The vintage art and chair were found at a flea market.

About Kristi Westlake, Allied ASID, LEED AP

Kristi Westlake, a "Georgia Peach," was born and raised in Newnan, Georgia, a small town just south of Atlanta. After graduating from The Art Institute of Atlanta, she founded Westlake Design Studio. Always striving for a new and better way, Kristi continued her education by researching green design and achieving her LEED Accreditation. Incorporating sustainable practices into her design approach allows her to introduce innovative alternatives to interior spaces. Kristi integrates sustainable practices into every project by carefully analyzing the space, its occupants, and the activities performed in the space. Materials and products are carefully considered with regard to their effects on the end user and the environment. Westlake Design Studio was recently featured in the 2008 Woodbury Christmas Tour of Homes.

Westlake Design Studio
30 Claret Court
Newnan, GA 30265
www.westlakedesignstudio.com

Barry home by SoCal Contractor, photos by Roi Yerushalmi

BARRY HOME BY SOCAL CONTRACTOR

In this kitchen and bath remodel the clients wanted a more efficient, easier to use, eco-friendly, and attractive "face lift" on spaces that had not been updated in thirty years. Many green materials were included, like European cabinetry with E1 emissions standards, CaesarStone countertops, reclaimed oak floors, Energy Star appliances, no-VOC paints, color-corrected fluorescent lighting, recycled content

tiles, and Water Sense fixtures. To improve natural light and airflow, a wall was removed in the kitchen and energy-efficient windows were installed in both rooms. The clients were given instructions on how to clean the spaces with non-toxic, earth-friendly products and encouraged to recycle food scraps and materials in a waste station with separate compartments for compost, recyclables, and trash. The clients also removed asbestos and installed an energy-efficient heating and ventilation system throughout the home, improving air quality and reducing energy loads and expenses.

GREENBLATT HOME BY SOCAL CONTRACTOR

Plans for this whole-house remodel included installation of green appliances, materials, and systems for energy conservation. The majority of the home faces southwest and consists of large windows causing tremendous amounts of heat transfer, resulting in the air conditioning having to work overtime. Since the home is built on a hillside it is nearly impossible to shade the house with trees or landscaping. The solution was to install properly sealed Low E3 windows and ceiling fans to circulate air. (During phase two the semitransparent Mecho shades will be installed allowing the light to come in but providing privacy and extra protection against the UV rays during the hottest hours of the day.)

Throughout the home, carbonized bamboo flooring and no-VOC paint were used. In the kitchen, European cabinets with E1 emission standards, fluorescent lighting, Water Sense fixtures, CaesarStone, and Energy Star Rated appliances were installed. The old cabinets were removed and installed in the garage for additional storage. The appliances were recycled and donated. In the dining room recycled-glass pendant lights were installed over the vintage dining table. Previously the office was a very dark space that needed artificial illumination

Greenblatt home by SoCal Contractor, photos by Roi Yerushalmi

throughout the day. Removing a wall allowed natural light to flood the space. Eldorado stone brick veneer was added to a large wall in the living room transforming the look from tract home to urban loft. The client was an environmental advocate prior to selecting SoCal Contractor to renovate his home, but promised to recycle and used eco-friendly cleaning products.

About SoCal Contractor

Roi Yerushalmi, owner of SoCal Contractor, is a licensed contractor and an avid surfer and snowboarder who loves being in nature. He grew up on

Barry home by SoCal Contractor, photos by Roi Yerushalmi

a kibbutz in Israel that held conservationism and environmentalism as part of its core values. At a very young age he began working with his father in construction and was put in charge of the landscaping services for the village. They didn't have a special name for the way they approached the built environment, instead they just used techniques and products that didn't waste or pollute. When he came to the United States he learned that most builders did not have such an eco-friendly way of doing things and that he had, in fact, spent an entire life and career being green. When he started SoCal Contractor, he focused on being a full-service green building and remodeling company that implements the latest technology and building techniques to minimize costs and impact on the environment. They use recyclable, sustainable, and earth-friendly materials, methods, and products, taking construction into the 21st century. Their work has been featured in *Home Magazine*, *Icon*, *LA Design*, *Angeleno*, *Small Room Decorating*, *Apartment Therapy*, and *Design*Sponge*. The company also donates a portion of its profits to Surfrider Foundation and World Wildlife Fund.

www.SoCalContractor.com

Greenblatt home by SoCal Contractor, photos by Roi Yerushalmi

ABOUT THE AUTHOR

Lori Dennis is the founder and principal of Lori Dennis, Inc., a firm specializing in green, sustainable interior design since 1998. Dennis' eco-friendly projects include residential, commercial, and hospitality interiors in Beverly Hills, Los Angeles, Miami, Palm Springs, and New York. She is a member of the American Society of Interior Designers (ASID) and serves on ASID's Green Committee.

In 2007 she passed the USGBC Leadership in Energy and Environmental Design Exam to become a LEED AP. Her firm has won numerous green awards including the *Home Magazine* Award for Best Green Remodel, the *Southern Accents*/ASID National Award for Best Green Interior Design, the *California Homes*/ASID Award for Best Green Interior Design, the Viking Best Kitchen Design award, and the *Angeleno Magazine*/ASID Award for Best Modern Interior Design.

Dennis, a graduate of the UCLA Interior Design program, has had designs featured in *Woman's Day Magazine*, *Coastal Living*, *Southern Accents*, *Home Magazine*, *Smart Home Owner*, *HGTV Magazine*, *Small Room Decorating*, *Los Angeles Times*, *The New York Times*, *Apartment Therapy*, *People* magazine, *Dwell*, and countless other magazines and Web sites around the world. She has been a guest expert on HGTV, Food Network, Oxygen Network, NBC, XM radio, and KABC Radio Los Angeles, and has lectured on green interior design at UCLA, FIDM Los Angeles Campus, Design Within Reach, Dwell on Design, Alt Build, and Westweek at the Pacific Design Center. She contributes to Tibetsi.com, *KBB Green Magazine*, and writes her own blog called *Glamorous Green*.

Green interior design is more than a profession to Lori Dennis—it is a passion. Her desire to be part of the solution to waste and pollution in the interior design and construction fields led her to write this book. Dennis shares her secrets with the hope that she will help thousands of people easily make the transition to a greener way of life.

INDEX

Books From Allworth Press

Allworth Press is an imprint of Allworth Communications, Inc. Selected titles are listed below.

Green Graphic Design
by Brian Dougherty with Celery Design Collaborative
(6 x 9, 212 pages, paperback, $24.95)

Interior Design Practice
by Cindy Coleman
(6 x 9, 256 pages, paperback, $24.95)

Marketing Interior Design
by Lloyd Princeton
(6 x 9, 224 pages, paperback, $24.95)

Interior Design Clients
by Thomas L. Williams
(6 x 9, 234 pages, paperback, $24.95)

Starting Your Career as an Interior Designer
by Robert K. Hale and Thomas L. Williams
(6 x 9, 240 pages, paperback, $24.95)

Interior Designer's Guide to Pricing, Estimating, and Budgeting, Second Edition
by Theo Stephan Williams
(6 x 9, 208 pages, paperback, $24.95)

Business and Legal Forms for Interior Designers
by Tad Crawford and Eva Doman Bruck
(8 1/2 x 11, 208 pages, paperback, $29.95)

How to Start and Operate Your Own Design Firm: A Guide for Interior Designers and Architects
by Albert W. Rubeling
(6 x 9, 256 pages, paperback, $24.95)

The Challenge of Interior Design: Professional Values and Opportunities
by Mary V. Knackstedt
(6 x 9, 272 pages, paperback, $24.95)

How to Start a Faux Painting or Mural Business, Second Edition
by Rebecca Pittman
(6 x 9, 240 pages, paperback, $24.95)

Emotional Branding, Revised Edition
by Marc Gobé
(6 x 9, 360 pages, paperback, $19.95)

Designers Don't Read
by Austin Howe
(5 1/2 x 8 1/2, 224 pages, paperback, $24.95)

POP: How Graphic Design Shapes Popular Culture
by Steven Heller
(6 x 9, 296, paperback, $24.95)

How to Think Like a Great Graphic Designer
by Debbie Millman
(6 x 9, 248 pages, paperback, $24.95)

To request a free catalog or order books by credit card, call 1-800-491-2808. To see our complete catalog on the World Wide Web, or to order online, please visit *www.allworth.com.*